THE
TERRIBLE TRIO

Tributes

'They always appeared to play as one. Their individual skills, expertise, positional sense and scoring ability were simply dovetailed into one unit.'

— Tommy Walker, in *Glorious Hearts*

'They linked beautifully, there must have been some kind of chemistry between them.'

— Alex Young, in *Hearts Greats*

'Nobody compared with Conn, Bauld and Wardhaugh in attack. They were a great threesome and the biggest influence on the team.'

— John Cumming, in *Hearts Greats*

'There were not many better players than Conn, Bauld and Wardhaugh and, as a threesome, they were untouchable.'

— The Author of *Hearts Greats*

THE TERRIBLE TRIO

Brian Scott

SPORTSPRINT PUBLISHING
EDINBURGH

ISBN 0 85976 306 4

Phototypeset by Beecee Typesetting Services
Printed in Great Britain by Bell & Bain Ltd., Glasgow

Profiles

CONN, Alfie (1944-58)

Born: Prestonpans, 2.10.1926
Previous club: Inveresk Ath
Height: 5ft 7in
Weight: 11st 6lbs
Club appearances: 407
Goals: 219
International appearances:
1949 v Irish League;
1955 v English League;
1956 v Danish League and Austria

BAULD, William Russell Logan (1946-62)

Born: Newcraighall, Edinburgh, 24.1.1928
Died: 11.3.1977
Previous club: Musselburgh Ath
Height: 5ft 8in
Weight: 11st 4lbs
Club appearances: 510
Goals: 356
International appearances:
1950 v England, Portugal and Switzerland, English League and Irish League; 1952 v Irish League and League of Ireland; 1954 v English League and Irish League; 1955 v League of Ireland; 1957 v English League and Irish League; 1958 v Irish League and League of Ireland; 1959 v English League and League of Ireland.

WARDHAUGH, James (1946-59)

Born: Marshall Meadows, Berwick, 21.3.1929
Died: 2.1.1978
Previous club: Shaftesbury Park
Height: 5ft 8in
Weight: 10st 6lbs
Club appearances: 517
Goals: 375
International appearances:
1951 v League of Ireland; 1952 v Irish League; 1955 v Hungary, English League, Irish League and League of Ireland; 1956 v Danish League and English League; 1957 v Northern Ireland, League of Ireland and Irish League

Acknowledgements

More than forty years have elapsed since Alfie Conn, Willie Bauld and Jimmy Wardhaugh united to become The Terrible Trio, and I congratulate Tynecastle colleagues, Davie Laing and Fred Glidden, for being able to remember that far back!

I am indebted to them as well as to Mrs Ann Wardhaugh for their help in piecing together the Trio's colourful tale as well as former players Tommy Gallacher and George Hill (Dundee), Doug Baillie (Airdrie), John Urquhart, Alex Young, John Cumming and Alan Gordon (Hearts) and Eddie Turnbull (Hibs).

My grateful thanks are due, too, to fellow journalists Stewart Brown, Alex Cameron, Jim Black and Jim Masson, for aiding my research; also to David Thomson of the Scottish Football League.

I am especially grateful to D.C. Thomson and Company and to Alan Gordon for illustrations, and to the *Sunday Post*, *Scottish Daily Express*, *Scottish Daily Mail*, *Edinburgh Evening News* and *Daily Record*, for the opportunity to sift through their files.

B.S.

Contents

CHAPTER ONE

Truly Terrible

'Terrible' tends to be a misused word but, in its strictest sense, it aptly described the Trio which was Conn, Bauld and Wardhaugh. These three players really did inspire terror among opposing defences, earning a reputation within Scottish football and an affection at Tynecastle which still endures.

Hearts' history is all the more enriched by the deeds of their most famous post-war forwards who, between them, scored almost 1,000 goals during the club's most successful era.

When Stewart Brown of the Edinburgh *Evening News* tagged John Colquhoun, John Robertson and Scott Crabbe as the New Terrible Trio, he effectively challenged them to reach for a standard of excellence which seems impossible to surpass.

Conn, Bauld and Wardhaugh were endowed with varying gifts which, when parcelled together, made them arguably the most exciting offering ever placed before a Scottish crowd.

True, Hibs could boast about their Famous Five of Smith, Johnstone, Reilly, Turnbull and Ormond but Hearts' Terrible Trio contrived, with an economy of numbers, to achieve at least as much celebrity.

Alfie Conn, Willie Bauld and Jimmy Wardhaugh were bequeathed to Hearts by Davie McLean, a manager whose astuteness in the matter of team building became widely recognised only after his death in 1951.

Under the stewardship of his greatly respected successor, Tommy Walker, in the 1950s, McLean's dream for Hearts turned

1

into reality as trophies, each reflecting the talents of the Trio, began to materialise at Tynecastle for the first time in almost half a century.

'A club could spend millions of pounds nowadays and not strike as successful a partnership as Alfie, Willie and Jimmy had going,' recalled the estimable Davie Laing, another prodigy of McLean's and a wing-half in the side which emerged from the Second World War with such great aspirations.

'Each of them was a top-class player in his own right but the secret of their success as a trio was in their blend. They clicked together as if by magic. As a combination, they were as near to being perfect as you could have imagined.'

Analysing their differing qualities, Davie went on, 'Alfie was a strong-running player with a good turn of speed and a great, long-range shot. We used to say that, if Alfie scored from inside the box, it was unusual and that, if Jimmy scored from outside, it was a miracle.

'Jimmy, you see, had the knack of arriving in the penalty area at precisely the right time. "Twinkle-toes" we called him because he was also a great dribbler as well as a true grafter. Jimmy could run all day.

'Willie never wasted his effort, and yet he would also arrive at the right spot at exactly the right time. He was a tremendous finisher with his head or either foot.'

Such sentiments echoed throughout the Scottish game, not just at Tynecastle, which makes it all the harder to understand why Conn, Bauld and Wardhaugh won such scant recognition at international level.

Alfie's collection of honours amounted to one full cap and three League caps which, though, were prestigious enough in their day; Willie's to three and 13 (although injuries deprived him of many more) and Jimmy's to two and nine.

'The fact that such talented players won such a piffling amount of honours really put the selection process of the day into perspective,' Davie Laing argued. 'The selectors used to travel all over England picking players at random when they had better ones at home.

'At Tynecastle was a Trio which was second to none, yet not

Alfie Conn: ' . . . a strong-running player with a good turn of speed and a great, long-range shot.'

only did they fail to get the recognition they deserved as individuals, they never once played together for Scotland.

'Mind you, I can recall another example of such oversight. I once played for the Scottish League at Parkhead in a match for which four of Hibs' Famous Five were selected. Instead of going the whole way and naming Eddie Turnbull as well, the selectors chose Billy Steel of Dundee. It didn't make sense although Steel was a fine player.'

Alfie Conn was first to arrive at Tynecastle, as a 17-year-old in 1944 after learning the rudiments of his inside-forward craft with Bathgate Academy, Prestonpans YMCA and Inveresk Athletic.

Another former clubmate, Freddie Glidden, who captained the 1956 Scottish Cup-winning team, was his schoolmate in Bathgate, recalling, 'Even in those days, he had tremendous acceleration and used to win all the races at gala days and the likes.

'As a footballer, his talent was obvious from an early age and he later proved to be akin to Bobby Charlton in the way he could strike the ball with such power.'

Born into a mining family in Prestonpans, and moving to West Lothian and back during his youth, Alfie himself was lowered into the gloom of the pits as a so-called Bevin Boy to help the war effort.

On a typical match day, he would go on shift at 5 a.m. and not see daylight until shortly after noon, with time only to wash off the morning's grime and catch a bus to Edinburgh, arriving breathless in the Tynecastle dressing room about 45 minutes before kick-off.

He had already sampled first-team football by the time that Willie Bauld, also a Bevin Boy, signed for Hearts in May, 1946, as an 18-year-old after his registration with Sunderland had been cancelled.

But there was no instant promotion for Willie who, from the Newcraighall area, was farmed out first to Newtongrange Star, then Edinburgh City in the Scottish C Division to add to the experience he had gained with Edinburgh Waverley and Musselburgh Union.

Coincidentally, the aforementioned Freddie Glidden played behind him at Newtongrange which was Hearts' nursery in those days and remembered, 'Even in those days, he had everything. He was as lethal with one foot as the other and seemed able to hang in the air when anybody sent a cross over in his direction.'

Jimmy Wardhaugh, born at a dot on the map near Berwick, Marshall Meadow, was recruited by Hearts from Shaftesbury Park precisely one month before Willie. He had already established a football reputation with the Air Training Corps, having captained them in an international tournament in Geneva earlier in 1946.

Jimmy Wardhaugh: ' . . . a great dribbler as well as a true grafter. Jimmy could run all day.'

Something of an all-rounder, the then 17-year-old Jimmy had played rugby at school and was also a keen cricketer and, later, a fan of ice hockey about which he was to write for an Edinburgh evening newspaper.

But his versatility was shared by the two men with whom he was to achieve such esteem at Tynecastle for, like so many footballers, they were also blessed with the co-ordination which allowed them to strike any ball with style and precision.

Alfie, for example, was a match for most at golf, billiards and table tennis, while Willie played golf and even the occasional game of cricket with considerable verve.

Indeed, before he could afford to buy his own clubs, the naturally left-handed Willie tired of trying to borrow a set to suit. So, to the surprise of his partners, he changed to a right-handed grip and played on like a champion.

The Hearts to which the Trio were introduced as novice professionals had not won a trophy since the distant days of 1906 and Davie McLean was charged with the task of blowing away the cobwebs which clung to the club's display cabinet. He had assembled a fine Scottish Cup-winning side at East Fife in the late 1930s and, in the early war years which followed, was invited to carry his alchemist's touch across the Forth Bridge to Tynecastle.

His ethic was to find good young players and wean them towards maturity, so he made a start by signing such as Jimmy Brown, Ken Currie, Jack Dewar and Davie Laing in 1942.

'We had played with Bayview Youth Club which Davie McLean set up as a nursery for East Fife,' Davie Laing remembered. 'As such we were expected to sign for East Fife. Instead, we went to Tynecastle as Davie McLean's boys and that meant we got a rough reception any time we played at Bayview.

'Tommy McKenzie, Bobby Dougan and Archie Kelly were others signed around that time, so the foundations were laid for the future. Really, it was a super atmosphere in which to be reared as, I'm sure, Alfie, Willie and Jimmy would have agreed.'

But Tynecastle fans were notoriously impatient and, when success was still not in prospect by season 1947-48, McLean went against his instincts by making an unprecedented plunge into the transfer market.

Bobby Flavell, Arthur Dixon and George Hamilton were signed in a £23,000 package although Hearts politely declined Hibs' kind offer of taking a couple of players, including the very young Willie Ormond, on loan.

Uncomfortable though their plight was — they were bottom of the League in January 1948 — Hearts could not be seen to accept charity from their city rivals.

That rather traumatic season, during which the Shareholders' Association questioned the stewardship of the club and McLean offered to resign, ended with Hearts achieving a hint of respectability by finishing in 9th position.

Willie Bauld: ' . . . never wasted his effort, and yet he would also arrive at the right spot at exactly the right time . . . a tremendous finisher with his head or either foot.'

Alfie Conn had been out for several months by then with a cartilage injury, although he had given more than a hint of his scoring potential in more than a dozen League and Cup games the previous season.

Jimmy Wardhaugh had also shown considerable promise during 1946-47 but the big-money signings seemed to consign both him and Alfie to the reserves once more in order to complete their apprenticeships.

Willie Bauld, of course, was still virtually unknown to Hearts fans unless, that is, they scrutinised the small print of local newspapers to check on his progress with the now-defunct Edinburgh City.

Following his season at Newtongrange, he had been loaned to City which, in the sceptical view of many Hearts players, suggested that he was on the verge of a free transfer. Who is to say that he would not have got one if season 1948-49 had begun more successfully than it did?

In fact, it began with the news which had been denied during the summer — that Tommy Walker was shortly to return from Chelsea after his widely-publicised, two-year sojourn there. But Hearts fans found little else to cheer as the team, featuring a forward line of McFarlane, Currie, Flavell, Dixon and Williams lost to Dundee at Dens Park.

Alfie Conn and Willie Bauld, meanwhile, were in the reserves on that opening day and Jimmy Wardhaugh joined Willie in the second team which played a Rangers Select at the opening of Broxburn Athletic's ground the following midweek. Thus it was an inauspicious start to the season for the Trio as well as the Hearts' first team who proceeded to take only two points from their opening six League matches.

Alfie was promoted along with several others in a vain attempt to arrest their bad run of results but, after a defeat by Celtic, the Edinburgh *Evening News* commented rather sourly, 'The mere substitution of one set of mediocre players for another is pointless. Only Laing had a sound game.'

By September, Hearts' hope was that the League Cup would bring them a change of luck, but it was their misfortune to be drawn in the same group as the holders, East Fife, and they suffered a 4-0 thrashing at Bayview after starting the tournament with a draw against Partick Thistle.

Still, Alfie was holding his place in the team and, with Bobby Flavell having lodged a transfer request, the *Evening News* suggested helpfully that the young reserve, Wardhaugh, 'might be entrusted with the centre-forward position'.

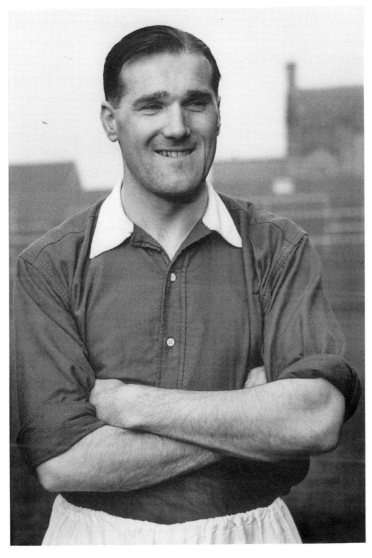

A valuable team-mate for the Trio would be Tommy McKenzie, signed by Davie McLean in the '40s build-up.

Davie McLean declined the advice, however. He even omitted Alfie for the following match, a win over Queen of the South at Palmerston, and retained his selection for the away tie with Partick Thistle which resulted in defeat.

The manager, fighting off accusations of 'chopping and changing his team too much', managed to contain his anguish.

But he sensed that still more changes, possibly sweeping ones, had to be made if Hearts were to cope with East Fife's challenge at Tynecastle the following Saturday, October 9.

So, he called for a report on the reserves' performance against Partick Thistle and began to toy with the names of a few youngsters who might just be ready for first-team duty. Since Hearts were as good as out of the League Cup anyway, he could probably afford to experiment.

Certainly, Hearts fans deserved tastier fare than they had been served by that point in the season, but it is doubtful if their palates watered when they read the brief intimation in Thursday's papers that Conn, Bauld and Wardhaugh were in Hearts' squad of 14 players to face East Fife . . .

CHAPTER TWO

Trio take their Bow

Willie Bauld blanched that second Saturday in October as he strolled up Dalry Road towards Tynecastle after eating a light lunch at the Haymarket.

'Whae's this mug the Hearts hiv got playin' at centre-forward the day, then?' he overheard one disillusioned fan demand of another.

Willie's face was virtually unknown of course, and the question pinched his nerves which had been tingling ever since he was told to stand by for first-team duty in the company of Alfie and Jimmy.

But he needn't have worried, for, after just 14 minutes of his outstanding debut against East Fife, he scored the first of his 356 goals for the Edinburgh side, from a perfect cross by winger Tommy Sloan.

After 64 minutes, the 20-year-old claimed his second and, 10 minutes later, his third. For a man soon to be crowned the King of Hearts, his was truly a regal entrance.

That memorable match marked the formation of the Terrible Trio and, just to ensure that he, too, got an honourable mention in the Sunday papers, Alfie scored twice.

A penalty by Davie Laing completed the unpredicted, 6-1 trouncing of the Bayview team who, remember, had beaten Hearts by 4-0 at home only three weeks earlier.

But Hearts were a team transformed in terms of personnel, their forward line completely recast to include Sloan, left-winger Archie Williams as well as the youthful Conn, Bauld and Wardhaugh.

Not only that, but manager McLean had moved Bobby Parker to right-back, thus signalling the start of another sterling partnership in the emergent Tynecastle team, that of Parker and left-back Tommy McKenzie.

Bobby Dougan came in at centre-half and, according to both Davie Laing and Alfie Conn, his soothing presence gave Hearts yet another dimension.

'Bubbling over with enthusiasm, Hearts played East Fife to a standstill,' the *Evening News* reported. 'The score in no way flattered the winners.' Of the blond-haired Bauld, the bulletin went on, 'He made an auspicious start by getting a hat-trick. If not a polished leader, he used his weight and speed to good effect and held the attack together well.'

Ironically, Bauld was soon to be recognised throughout Scotland as a very polished leader, one who relied on wiles rather than weight and who wasn't greatly endowed with speed. Nonetheless, he probably appreciated the *News* scribe's thoughtful tribute.

Needless to say, the Tynecastle crowd dispersed that afternoon with certain reason for optimism. They had caught a glimpse of Hearts' future and liked the look of it.

Midway through the following week, Davie McLean promised that he would field an unchanged team against Queen of the South, just so long as young Bauld recovered from the cold which had seen him confined to bed for a couple of days.

Come the Saturday, he was fit to play and fit to rattle in another three goals, his ally Alfie getting the fourth in a splendid 4-0 victory before a disbelieving crowd of 32,000.

So it was that Hearts, sustained by the deeds of their newly-formed trio of forwards, approached the following Saturday's match with Rangers. It marked the resumption of the League, of which the Tynecastle team were still bottom, but the talk was not so much about their chance of winning as Willie's hope of scoring a third, successive hat-trick. A new confidence had quickly been bred amongst Hearts fans!

In the event, Willie fired only blanks, although Alfie shot a fine goal from the centre's pass while Jimmy Wardhaugh bulleted in a header to help record a creditable 2-0 victory over the Ibrox side.

Soon to be crowned the King of Hearts, Willie Bauld made an outstanding debut against East Fife by scoring three goals. Alfie Conn scored twice. The Terrible Trio was born

Rangers' apologists pointed to the fact that they were without both George Young and Willie Waddell who were on international duty in Wales, but this fact was happily overlooked by Hearts supporters who truly believed that the new era had dawned.

They were not discouraged from their view by the *Evening News* which enthused about 'this bustling, try-anything inside trio' of

Conn, Bauld and Wardhaugh, who, they predicted, 'are going to do a lot of damage before the season is out'.

The writer also enthused about Alfie's 'goal in a thousand' against Rangers; one which effectively propelled him into the Scottish League team to play the Irish League the following month.

Jimmy Wardhaugh was at that time doing his National Service in the RAF, travelling back to Scotland from Worcestershire every other Friday in order to play in a side which, alas, was still too immature to be consistent.

Despite two goals by Willie, for example, Hearts drew 3-3 with Clyde at Shawfield. Despite one apiece from Jimmy and Willie, they were beaten 5-3 by Falkirk at Brockville. Poor Willie was barracked at half-time there but the fans forgave him the instant that he laid on Jimmy's goal.

It was time for Davie McLean to take stock once more. His team were still bottom of the League, after all, with only five points from 10 matches. But he sensed that they would soon begin to claw their way upwards — which they did on the strength of goals by Willie, Alfie and Jimmy in the three matches which followed.

Hearts were then in fourth bottom position, ready to tackle East Fife at home and prove with luck, that that 6-1 victory in the League Cup just two months earlier had been no fluke. This they did with ease, winning by a convincing 4-0 with Willie and Alfie scoring once and Tommy Sloan twice.

'Nothing is any bother to this boy Bauld,' the *Sunday Post* recorded and, after Jimmy had bagged his first-ever hat-trick for the club against Jock Stein's Albion Rovers, the same paper enthused about 'the outstanding work of Bauld' following his Christmas goal against Third Lanark.

An auspicious New Year seemed to beckon, the old one having yielded much promise, but Hearts fans had something other than the outstanding emergence of Conn, Bauld and Wardhaugh to chatter about as they prepared to toast the arrival of 1949. Tommy Walker was on his way back at last, both as a player and an assistant to Davie McLean.

Something akin to a royal reception was arranged for Tommy's arrival at Waverley Station from London. Then the word got out that he planned a much more modest return, journeying up by car but still in time to see the Ne'erday derby with Hibs at Tynecastle.

It turned out to be a grand occasion, Tommy being welcomed with a chorus of 'For he's a jolly good fellow' when he arrived for the match accompanied by his wife and young son.

He had heard good reports about the new and exciting young Hearts players although his knowledge of Alfie's potential was first-hand since they had played together several times before Tommy's move south.

In the event, Alfie scored a fine and dramatically-timed winning goal against Hibs, taking a pass from Willie in the last minute and swerving through their defence to ram the ball past Jimmy Kerr. Willie and Bobby Flavell, with Jimmy Wardhaugh's cunning assistance, had scored in the first 20 minutes to set the Tynecastle side up for their 3-2 victory which underscored the belief that 1949 would be a good year.

Davie McLean's hope was that the unmatched experience of Tommy Walker would act as a catalyst on the field, speeding up the maturing process of his young players. So he slotted him in at right-half against Dundee.

Alas, the game did not go Hearts' way and a late positional switch involving Tommy and Alfie failed to save them from a 1-0 defeat.

It was shortly afterwards that manager McLean called Tommy aside and told him: 'Perhaps you should sit beside me in future rather than play. It will be difficult for you to point out mistakes in others if you make some yourself'.

The inference was that Tommy was past his best, but he accepted the situation and had agreed to stop playing by the time that Chelsea manager, Billy Birrell, made a goodwill visit to Scotland to see Hearts play St Mirren.

That match marked the start of a month's absence through injury of Alfie but Hearts contrived to win 2-1 with goals by Willie Bauld, from a pass by Jimmy Wardhaugh, and Bobby Flavell.

Still without Alfie, they launched sucessfully into the Scottish Cup, beating Airdrie 4-1 with Jimmy scoring twice and Willie once. Then they turned over Motherwell, Jimmy and Willie both scoring in an entertaining 5-1 win at Tynecastle.

Alfie duly returned for the third round of the Cup, scoring one of the goals in a 3-0 win over Dumbarton. Jimmy had done likewise as Third Lanark went down by 3-1 in the previous round.

Thus, while it was impossible for Hearts to make their mark in the League that season, they seemed to have a realistic chance of winning the Cup for the first time in 42 years.

Indeed, their optimism was heightened when, thanks to Tommy Sloan and Charlie Cox, they led Dundee by 2-1 at half-time in the fourth-round tie at Dens Park. But the home side battled back manfully, forcing the tie into extra time and winning 4-2 after Davie Laing had missed a penalty claimed by Alfie.

That defeat left Hearts with little other than self-esteem to play for, and their results in the remaining weeks of the season were mixed, although the Trio continued to score on a regular enough basis.

Willie, in fact, bagged a first-half hat-trick in a 7-1 home win over Albion Rovers, although Jimmy, in only half a minute, and Alfie in nine, contrived to be on target before him.

The season ended with Hearts in eighth position which, assuredly, was progress. In Conn, Bauld and Wardhaugh they had discovered a partnership which would ensure that that progress reached a sparkling conclusion.

To a degree, it had been formed in desperation and Davie Laing mused, 'To think that the player we recalled in haste from Edinburgh City turned out to be *the* Willie Bauld! Amazing, wasn't it? Mind you, I would like to think that the half-back line of Cox, Dougan and Laing helped push them on. We tried to do our bit so that Alfie, Willie and Jimmy could enjoy their freedom up front.'

By way of writing a postscript to the Trio's first season together, Willie played in the reserve Cup Final against Hibs, which resulted in a 3-2 win for the Easter Road side. Two of their goals were scored by Jim Souness, another name which was to be etched in the Tynecastle legend.

A splendid tradition of those days was the annual, pre-season match between an Edinburgh Select and a top English side. Alfie and Willie were honoured to be chosen for that in August 1949, against Wolves.

Another partnership to emerge was that of Bobby Parker at right-back with Tommy McKenzie at left-back.

Alfie, with Gordon Smith playing to his right, found himself in direct opposition to the celebrated England international, Billy Wright, yet contrived to score both Edinburgh's goals in their 3-2 defeat.

Smith, incidentally, was being coveted at that time by another noted English team, Newcastle, although he was to remain at

Easter Road for another ten years — before transferring to Hearts. More of that much later.

Hearts' concentration in August 1949 was all too briefly on the League Cup; this, despite the fact that Willie scored a hat-trick both home and away against sectional opponents, Stirling Albion.

By the turn of the year he was to rattle another four past the same opponents in a League game at Annfield, to ensure that they shivered at the mere mention of his name. But Hearts had several results to savour before then, the tastiest of them being a 5-2 win over Hibs who had been champions the previous year.

Alfie and Willie claimed two goals each on that derby occasion at Tynecastle whilst Jimmy rifled four past Clyde in a subsequent 6-2 victory. It seemed then that everything the Trio touched turned to goals — Jimmy scoring two out of a spectacular nine against Falkirk, Jimmy and Alfie sharing four against Aberdeen.

All the while, Hearts were spiralling up the table and they reached second top position when Willie scored twice in a 4-2 win over Celtic at Parkhead on the last day of the year.

Imagine, then, how confident they were when they took on Hibs at Easter Road in the derby game on January 2. It was a nerve-tingling encounter, Hearts edging it by 2-1 with Alfie and Jimmy scoring their goals.

Tommy Muirhead, the *Scottish Daily Express's* much-respected correspondent and, of course, former international player, nominated Alfie as his man of the match for a performance which he described as 'well-nigh perfect'.

Willie, who was already catching the eye of the Scotland selectors, picked up an injury and missed the 5-0 win over St Mirren. But he was fit again and in fine form by February when he scored a hat-trick in a 4-3 win over Clyde at Shawfield.

The great debate then was who would be Scotland's centre-forward for the crucial match with England at Hampden in April 1950, the result of which would determine whether or not Scotland participated in the World Cup Finals for the first time.

Lawrie Reilly of Hibs was preferred as an outside-left by the selectors so they toyed with the names of Bauld, Paddy Buckley of St Johnstone and Neil Mochan of Morton as an alternative to Queen of the South's Billy Houliston, who was injured.

Bauld, having begun his representative career with a hat-trick for the Scottish League against the Irish League at Ibrox, continued to underline his claim with two goals against Houliston's side and three against Stirling Albion.

Then, the week before the international, he claimed another hat-trick in a 5-0 win over Aberdeen at Pittodrie to persuade the selectors that he should replace the burly Houliston who had finally been discounted on fitness grounds.

So it was that, with Hearts still clinging to third place in the League and having avenged their Scottish Cup defeat by Aberdeen, their starlet centre-forward went to Hampden to confront the greatest challenge of his young career. The match was billed as the Game of the Century although Clyde and Celtic fans seemed not to acknowledge the fact, 25,000 of them turning out to see their teams in opposition at Shawfield on the same day, April 15.

Doubtless, Willie was anxious. John Cumming was to recall much later that his habit before games was to disappear into the 'smallest room' and drag on a cigarette to soothe his nerves.

Fielded in a forward line of Waddell (Rangers), Moir (Bolton), Steel (Derby) and Liddell (Liverpool), he seemed ill at ease as the match began, kicking the ground instead of the ball when an early scoring chance presented itself.

Then, after Roy Bentley of Chelsea had given England a 1-0 lead which they were to hold to the end, he struck a knee-high shot past the post and struck the bar with his final effort.

Yet while he blamed himself for the defeat, others were kinder in their appraisal of his full international debut, the *Sunday Post* reporting that he and Liddell were the best of Scotland's forwards.

Hearts manager McLean observed astutely, too, that 'Willie played well without being played to', implying that his gifted young centre-forward didn't enjoy the kind of service to which he was by then accustomed with his club.

It is worth recording that, even in defeat, the Scots could have taken up an invitation to make up the 16 teams competing in the World Cup Finals. Pride prevented them from doing so, for they had vowed they would only go as Home International Champions.

Hearts had some unfinished business to attend to that season —
a League match against Dundee at Tynecastle — and Willie
quickly demonstrated that his Hampden misses were mere
aberrations by scoring a hat-trick in only seven, first-half minutes.

Jimmy Wardhaugh claimed another two goals before half-time
and Alfie one, Hearts going on to record a rousing 6-2 victory
which confirmed them as the third top team in the
Championship.

'Our manager, George Anderson, was "beeling" in the dressing
room during the interval that day,' Dundee's George 'Pud' Hill
recalled. 'Hearts were 6-1 up at that point and the Trio were
playing brilliantly. Bauld was a superb player, different from
Lawrie Reilly who was his great rival. Reilly was sharper whereas
Bauld played in a wider sphere, using the wings to fine effect.'

Pud's team-mate and lifelong friend, Tommy Gallacher, added,
'Alfie Conn, Willie Bauld and Jimmy Wardhaugh were
exceptional players and Bauld was brilliant. He was the only
player I knew who could trouble our Doug Cowie in the air.

'Jimmy had to be watched like a hawk because he was all over
the park. Alfie played a bit behind the other two and had a
tremendous shot. They were a good blend alright, and three nice
lads, too. Most teams then had a couple of hammer-throwers but
Conn, Bauld and Wardhaugh were concerned only with playing
football.'

CHAPTER THREE

Bauld: Scotland's Scapegoat

The summer of 1950 approached, with Willie Bauld counting himself fortunate in not having time to mope about what might have been in his international debut against England at Hampden.

Eleven days later he was back at the famous Glasgow ground to face Switzerland in a game which was to serve as a warm-up to Scotland's close-season trip to Portugal and France.

His confidence reinforced by his re-selection, and with his cultured club-mate, Bobby Dougan, for company in the side, Willie scored with a typical header, from a cross by Lawrie Reilly, after only nine minutes.

Switzerland had equalised when, in the 38th minute of the match, Hearts' young hero had a shot blocked but Bobby Campbell of Chelsea followed up to score a second goal for the Scots.

Then Allan Brown, soon to move from East Fife to Blackpool, as a right-wing partner for Stanley Matthews, claimed a third goal immediately before the interval to complete the 3-1 victory.

The *Scottish Daily Express* proclaimed in its headline the next morning: 'BAULD HAS COME TO STAY'. Thus, Willie was in good heart when the Scotland party set off to play Portugal a month later. A crowd of 60,000 crammed into the Lisbon stadium on May 25 for what turned out to be an exciting, competitive match, which ended in a 2-2 draw with Brown and Bauld claiming the visitors' goals.

But, amazingly, Scotland were slated for their performance although Tommy Muirhead opined in the *Express* that 'Bauld took his goal well and used the ball cleverly' — his only problem being that his inside-forward support of Brown and Billy Steel sometimes lagged 50 yards behind!

Team captain, George Young of Rangers, who deferred to nobody, deflected the criticism of the team towards the selectors, saying, 'We have won eight out of our last ten games. If the SFA had given us bigger bonuses, we would have won the other two.'

So it was a disgruntled Scottish party which headed quickly to Paris amid rumour that sweeping changes would be made for the match there on May 27. In the event, only two players lost their places — Willie Bauld and Bobby Evans who were replaced by Lawrie Reilly, hitherto preferred at outside-left, and Ian McColl.

Tommy Muirhead jumped to the defence of the Hearts player, arguing in his column that 'the dropping of young Bauld is tantamount to saying that he was responsible for the poor forward display in Lisbon which is not true'.

Still, the all-powerful selectors believed that the result against the French — a 1-0 victory — justified their decision, although nobody would have believed at the time that Willie Bauld had played his last full international for Scotland.

An assortment of injuries, coupled with the selectors' preference for the more zestful approach of Lawrie Reilly, counted against the Tynecastle forward for years to come.

But there were many in Edinburgh who held Bauld to be a better player than his Easter Road rival — a belief which may have been underwritten when the Terrible Trio was chosen to play between the Hibs wingers, Gordon Smith and Willie Ormond, in the 1950 pre-season charity match against Newcastle.

Willie scored for the Hearts/Hibs select and the great Jackie Milburn for Newcastle. Little more than a month later, Hearts emphasised their superiority in the city by recording the first of two derby wins over Hibs that season.

It was a season tinged with sadness by the death in February, 1951, of the popular and far-sighted manager, Davie McLean. Tommy Walker was officially elevated to his position, although he had been dealing with most playing matters for more than a year.

In 1950 Bauld received international honours against England, Switzerland and Portugal, scoring a goal in Lisbon.

It was, too, a season in which Jimmy Wardhaugh emerged as an international candidate, his goals coming in the steady flow which was eventually to establish him as Hearts' most prolific scorer with a breathtaking total of 375, including 206 in the League.

One of his best came in a 5-1 win over East Fife in which Alfie and Wille shared the other four. Taking a pass from Willie, Jimmy set off on a lung-bursting run which, according to the *Sunday Post*, 'never stopped until he had rounded goalkeeper Niven and thrashed the ball into the net'.

He registered another notable goal on a treacherous wintry surface at Morton, collecting Willie's pass and swerving past a succession of slithering defenders to blast the ball past the international 'keeper Jimmy Cowan.

But controversy surrounded Jimmy's selection to play for the Scottish League against the League of Ireland in January, 1951, just a couple of weeks after he and Willie had scored in the 2-2 draw with Celtic at Parkhead.

Having been born at Marshall Meadow, half a mile south of the border, he was by rights an Englishman. Or was he? The footballing authorities of both England and Scotland had an unwritten rule stating that the border was not defined by the mark on the map but the line of the Tweed.

Jimmy, they agreed, had been born on the northern side of the river, so he must be Scottish. Furthermore, they acknowledged that nearby Berwick Rangers were, in practice, a Scottish team, so anybody born north of Berwick had to be Scottish.

Not that Jimmy had entertained any doubts about his nationality. His father was Scottish, an army man who just happened to have been stationed in the border country when Jimmy appeared on the scene. As a family, they moved to Edinburgh before he was big enough to kick a football.

By the time of Jimmy's first international honour, Hearts had slipped out of the top three in the Championship and they made an uncertain start to the Scottish Cup in the humble surroundings of Alloa.

Two goals down after only 33 minutes, they looked to be headed towards an embarrassing exit from the tournament until Alfie Conn scored twice within the space of 90 seconds immediately prior to the interval. Only when Jimmy Wardhaugh scored a third goal midway through the second half did they start to feel at ease.

If there was a lesson to be learned from that tie, Hearts appeared not to absorb it in time for the second round — at the equally unfashionable venue of East Stirling where they trailed 1-0 at half-time.

But East Stirling's luck cracked when their stalwart centre-half, Willie Quinn, stood in the way of a power-driven shot by a Hearts newcomer, John Cumming, and had to be assisted off. Confronted by only 10 men, Hearts thrust forward again and again to win by 5-1 with two goals by Willie Bauld and one each by Jimmy Wardhaugh, Tam McKenzie and Tommy Sloan.

In season 1950-51 Jimmy Wardhaugh was emerging as Hearts' most prolific goalscorer. His eventual total was 375, including 206 in the League.

Rather more convincing in their performance that same Cup day were Hibs, who beat Rangers by 3-2 at Ibrox to end the Glasgow side's three-year reign as holders. Willie Maley, formerly the manager of Celtic and obviously not a man bound up by Old Firm prejudice, wrote a letter of condolence to Bill Struth of Rangers.

Whether or not the revered Ibrox manager replied is unknown. But Celtic's centre-forward, John McPhail, received a note from a mournful Rangers fan saying, 'Only Celtic can bring the Cup to the west this season. Best of luck'.

Celtic, it transpired, were drawn against Hearts in the next round and McPhail appeared to be sustained by those good wishes, for he scored the decisive goal in his side's 2-1 victory at Tynecastle after Alfie Conn had equalised an early score by Jock Weir. Goalkeeper George Hunter was carried shoulder-high from the field at the end, and Celtic proceeded all the way to Hampden, beating Motherwell in the Final.

In the League, other West of Scotland clubs proved less of a problem to Hearts. They thrashed Clyde 4-0 at Tynecastle with the Trio claiming a goal each, and went on to annihilate Morton by 8-0, also at home, Alfie scoring a hat-trick.

Almost as noteworthy as that result was a squandered chance by Willie. When a shot by Jimmy Wardhaugh dropped off Morton's cross-bar and bounced only a yard from goal, Hearts' celebrated centre-forward swung his boot and completely missed his kick.

Alas, on Cup Final day, Hearts were beaten 1-0 at home by Rangers and, while they picked up with a 4-2 win at Motherwell (Bauld 2, Cumming and Wardhaugh being their scorers), they had to settle for fourth position in the League — and a close-season tour of West Germany.

Alfie had visited that war-stricken country as a teenage professional with Hearts and highlighted his return by scoring once in the 3-3 draw with Stuttgart. Willie went one better, scoring twice as Hearts, cheered on by British and American servicemen, established a 3-0 lead at half-time.

But heavy defeats by Offenbach Kickers and Augsburg took some of the enjoyment out of what was then a rare trip abroad for the Tynecastle players.

Still, they had much to look forward to in the new season. The Trio and their team-mates who still included Davie Laing, Charlie Cox, Bobby Dougan and Bobby Parker were maturing into a significant force, strong enough to win a trophy perhaps.

Sadly, the League Cup quickly proved to be beyond them, although Willie contrived to achieve one notable feat in that tournament by scoring all five of Hearts' goals in a remarkable 5-5 draw with St Mirren at Love Street. Poor Alex Crowe of Saints only scored four!

Alfie claimed a hat-trick in the 3-1 win at home against the Paisley side before Hearts launched into their League programme with Jimmy scoring twice in a 3-1 win over East Fife. It is worth recording that a 25,000 crowd watched that match. Tynecastle gate figures were spiralling higher and higher.

Thanks to a goal by Alfie, Hearts settled for a 1-1 draw in the first of the season's derby matches, but they excelled a week later with a 3-1 win over Celtic at Parkhead.

Their former goalkeeper, Jack Harkness, reported the match for the *Sunday Post* and told his millions of readers that the trio of Conn, Bauld and Wardhaugh, who all scored, were 'a treat to watch'.

But after the three had each scored again in a fine 4-2 win over Dundee, whom the itinerant Bobby Flavell had joined after his prodigal return to Tynecastle from Bogota, Hearts' progress was arrested.

They lost both to St Mirren and Rangers and didn't begin to pick up the pace again until they beat Queen of the South and Motherwell on successive Saturdays in November with Alfie and Willie, at least, getting back on the goals standard.

Jimmy was out through injury, and replaced by the young Jimmy Whittle, when they drove into December, determined to close up on East Fife and Hibs at the top of the League.

They succeeded in doing so by beating Raith Rovers 4-2 at Tynecastle with goals by Whittle, former Rangers winger Eddie Rutherford (2) and Alfie. Then, with Jimmy back in the forward line, they knocked East Fife off their lofty perch with a 4-2 win at Bayview, Alfie getting two of their goals.

Better still was Hearts' performance against Airdrie at Tynecastle on the last Saturday of 1951. They won 6-1 with Jimmy and Willie, who had been out of the scoring frame since a 2-2 draw against Aberdeen at the start of the month, knocking in two goals each.

Thus, Hearts were in a challenging and confident mood for the Ne'erday visit to Easter Road — a fixture which, according to Jack Harkness, had 'taken over from Old Firm contests as the glamour derby of the year'.

Hibs, the reigning champions, were again the League leaders, having edged one point ahead of East Fife after 17 matches. Hearts were only three points adrift, so it isn't difficult to imagine the eagerness with which the contest was awaited by the rival factions of Edinburgh fans.

A crowd of around 65,000 was anticipated but, in the event, heavy snow (and the odd hangover, no doubt) slashed the attendance to 39,000. Those who stayed at home were, without doubt, the losers.

In only ten minutes, Alfie Conn collided with the Hibs goal-keeper, Tommy Younger, and limped out to the right wing where he was to spend the remainder of the match, effectively making up the numbers.

It was an upset which threatened the early momentum Hearts had built up with a steady flow of forward passes from the half-back line by Freddie Glidden and Davie Laing.

Yet, only seven minutes later, Jimmy Wardhaugh beat Jock Govan and John Paterson in the air to head the Tynecastle side in front. Shortly afterwards Willie Bauld inspired a second, ear-splitting roar amongst the visiting support by holding off a couple of challenges and shooting into the far corner of the net.

Tension teased the nerves of the Hearts players when Lawrie Reilly pulled a goal back for Hibs within 60 seconds but then, seven minutes before the interval, Willie made the score 3-1 by converting a cross by Eddie Rutherford, following an incisive pass by Freddie Glidden.

Hibs rallied bravely once more with the impish Reilly scoring their second soon after the interval, and Jimmy Brown proceeded to make a string of superb saves to deny the Easter Road side an equaliser.

While all this drama was unfolding, Alfie clashed with Gordon Smith near the touchline, the celebrated Hibs winger tumbling onto the track and having to be carried off.

Hibs fans were hardly appeased by the fact that Smith re-appeared some five minutes later. They booed Alfie each time the ball went anywhere near him until they were distracted first by a Reilly shot hitting the bar, then by a late penalty award to Hibs.

Eddie Turnbull elected to take the kick but contrived to ram it against the legs of Jimmy Brown. So Hearts were reprieved, retreating to Tynecastle as 3-2 winners and ready, no doubt, for a belated Ne'erday celebration.

Alas, they never got as close to Hibs again that League season, finishing fourth after drawing with Dundee and Rangers and losing unexpectedly at Morton, where Willie was injured and withdrawn from the Scotland side to play the British Army at Newcastle. Ominously, Lawrie Reilly took his place in what was effectively a trial for the annual fixture with England.

The Scottish Cup promised to be kinder to the Tynecastle team who, granted a bye in the first round, beat Raith Rovers in the second with a late goal which was both made and scored by Willie.

Airdrie were their next opponents, and a 2-2 draw at Broomfield, in which both Willie and Alfie scored, signalled an astonishing replay at Tynecastle, one which ended 6-4 in Hearts' favour in front of a 41,000 crowd.

Willie claimed three of the ten goals that afternoon, and, under a blaring headline which declared: 'THIS MAN BAULD IN A CLASS OF HIS OWN' — the *Scottish Daily Express's* reporter and former internationalist, Jimmy Carabine, insisted, 'If he is not chosen to play against England on April 5, it will be an injustice. He *was* Hearts' forward line.'

Poor Jimmy Wardhaugh was wrestling with form problems at that time and had been edged to outside-left to allow Jimmy Whittle to play alongside Alfie and Willie. Yet Hearts retained their collective confidence as they marched on Hampden for a semi-final meeting with Motherwell which attracted a 99,000 crowd, despite sleet and a howling wind. Only 23,000 were counted at Easter Road for the other tie that day, March 29, between Third Lanark and Dundee.

Hearts made an auspicious start, Alfie shooting the first goal via the underside of the bar from Eddie Rutherford's cross after just five minutes. While Jimmy Brown had to make several saves thereafter, including one from his old team-mate Tommy Sloan, Hearts' lead remained intact until the 63rd minute when a defensive mix-up allowed Jimmy Watson to equalise.

The replay date was set for April 7, two days after the Scotland-England match for which both Willie Bauld and Jimmy

Wardhaugh were named as reserves. Ironically, Jimmy was dropped by Hearts. This time it was Motherwell who took the early lead, Watson scoring for them in only five minutes. But Willie displayed outstanding ingenuity to set up Hearts' equaliser shortly afterwards. Tapping a free kick to Alfie, he dashed forward as the inside-right played the ball back to Bobby Parker.

At precisely the right moment, Bobby chipped the ball on to Willie who glanced it sideways with his head for Eddie Rutherford to score.

The crowd, this time counted at 80,000, gnawed at their fingernails for the remainder of the 90 minutes, plus an extra 30, but still there was no winner between Hearts and Motherwell, so a second replay date was set for 48 hours later.

Jimmy Wardhaugh was reinstated and a 59,468 crowd saw Alfie score for Hearts who, alas, wilted and went down by 3-1 to the side destined to win the trophy that season.

The moral of Hearts' Hampden story in season 1951-52 was that they possessed almost all the elements needed to succeed, but their efforts against Motherwell, and Airdrie beforehand, drained their resolve for their remaining League match, against relegation-threatened Third Lanark at Cathkin. Minus Alfie and Jimmy, they lost 4-0 and were subjected to a slow hand clap.

CHAPTER FOUR

Success comes closer

Conn, Bauld and Wardhaugh had been operating as the Terrible Trio for almost four years, in which time Hearts' League form had shown a marked improvement. Yet the club's search for silverware seemed never-ending.

Some critics suggested that the players were not quite as fit as they might have been although Tommy Walker had the most respected and popular of trainers in Johnny Harvey who, of course, was to manage the club in the 1960s.

Others suspected that the team was still a player or two short to exploit its full potential, and there may have been some validity in their belief also.

But with former Motherwell player, Donald MacLeod, having been appointed as Harvey's assistant, Hearts launched into season 1952-53 with renewed ambition — as stressed by a 5-0 League Cup win over Rangers at Tynecastle.

Alfie, Willie and Jimmy shared all five goals, the inside-forwards scoring two each, although later lapses prevented Hearts from qualifying from their group for the fifth year in succession.

Their League form soon proved to be just as mercurial — a 3-2 win at Third Lanark being followed by a 3-1 defeat at Easter Road, where Bobby Parker claimed their sole consolation with a late penalty.

Alfie and Willie missed that match through injury, and while they rejoined Jimmy in the team to play East Fife, another 3-1 defeat was recorded. Something had to be done. Something *was* done. Alfie and Jimmy were dropped along with Bobby Dougan and Eddie Rutherford.

They accepted their demotion with good grace, Alfie arguing that the team had to be settled — with or without some of its best-known names. But still Hearts stumbled from game to game.

A narrow win over Partick Thistle, in which Willie and Johnny Urquhart scored, was followed by a narrow defeat at Dundee. Then a slender home victory against Celtic brought in its wake a frustrating failure at Falkirk.

By the time that Hearts were crushed 3-0 at Pittodrie where, according to the *Sunday Post*, 'not even the wiles of Willie Bauld could weld them into a team', they had slipped to sixth bottom position in the League.

The eventual reinstatement of Alfie and Jimmy did not instantly rid them of the curse of inconsistency, as was shown the day Hearts played Clyde. Jimmy scored two goals, the team lost three. They and the Trio seemed to have lost their way and the 2-1 Ne'erday defeat at Easter Road further disorientated them.

When they went in against Airdrie at Broomfield two days later, Hearts were second bottom of the Division but skipper Bobby Parker believed that their luck would change and, miraculously, it did.

Johnny Urquhart and Jimmy both scored with half-hit shots in the opening ten minutes to post early notice of a 2-1 victory. Later in January Alfie scored in a 3-1 win at Motherwell which seemed to confirm that the team was rediscovering its sense of direction.

But Tommy Walker seemed unconvinced. He was reported to have met Clyde manager, Pat Travers, around that time with a view to buying goalscorer Billy McPhail as a rival for Willie whose turn it was now to be dropped.

One match he missed out on was a 1-1 draw with Dundee, Alfie claiming Hearts' goal. His pride having been pricked, Willie returned in the Scottish Cup tie at Raith Rovers the following week to score the only goal.

Despite the narrowness of the score at Stark Park, it was a match in which Hearts played especially well, as the *Sunday Post* was quick to acknowledge in the following terms: 'Wing-halves Armstrong and Laing were in complete command, with Conn

In season 1953-54 Jimmy was to score 27 goals in 28 Championship matches.

and Wardhaugh rejoicing in their service. Bauld completed a beautifully-moving machine.'

This seemed more like the Hearts of the previous season, and they proceeded to give another good account of themselves in the Cup by beating Montrose and Queen of the South in successive rounds, Willie scoring against the Angus club who were tagged as being 'the last of the rabbits'.

Given that they had begun the season with a 5-0 win over Rangers, Hearts had no reason to be pessimistic about the outcome of their semi-final tie with the Ibrox club who had beaten Celtic at the quarter-final stage.

But, in a pre-match interview, Rangers' Willie Woodburn warned Hearts not to believe it a good omen that the three teams they had beaten so far — Raith, Montrose and Queen of the South — all played in blue.

'Rangers will win', Woodburn asserted, and so they did with goals by Derek Grierson and John Prentice allowing them to overtake the 11th-minute lead which Jimmy Wardhaugh had given Hearts.

Mind you, the Ibrox side had to fight to the last for their victory, Willie Bauld heading past in the final minute after George Niven had thwarted him with a great save and Alfie Conn had had a shot cleared off the line by George Young.

Hearts' intervening form in the League had been much more encouraging than before the turn of the year, and no side suffered more as a result than Clyde who collapsed under a seven-goal battering at Tynecastle in late March.

Willie helped himself to a hat-trick that day with what were described as 'two bullet-like headers and a blistering drive', but Alfie missed a last-minute penalty after Jimmy had scored once and John Cumming twice in a brief, bewildering spell for the Shawfield team.

The King duly claimed another hat-trick, this time in a 4-2 win at Brockville, as the rejuventated Hearts finished the season in fourth top position for the third year in succession. They sensed that they could have done better and pledged themselves to prove it the following season, 1953-54.

It was one in which Jimmy excelled, with 27 goals in 28 Championship games, his best performance in eight seasons at Tynecastle. Ironically, he claimed many of those goals from the centre-forward position as Willie struggled to combat painful injuries to his back and knee.

An unfortunate consequence of Willie's fitness problems was that he missed out on a cap against Northern Ireland in October after impressing with two of the Scottish League's four goals against the Irish League at Ibrox.

Willie had warmed up for the season by scoring twice for the Edinburgh Select in their still-popular annual charity game, this time against Wolves. He was informally adopted as a member of

Hibs' Famous Five that day, spearheading an attack which included Gordon Smith, Bobby Johnstone, Eddie Turnbull and Willie Ormond.

Lawrie Reilly was in dispute with Hibs at the time and had taken a job as a rep for a paint firm. Thus, he missed out on the first of the derbies which resulted in a resounding 4-0 win for Hearts at Tynecastle. Alfie, Willie and Jimmy all scored on that occasion, as did Bobby Parker with a penalty.

Only one week previously, Hearts had lost 4-1 to Queen of the South at Tynecastle. Reilly was witness to their poor performance in his capacity as guest writer for the *Sunday Post* and his criticism may have stung the Hearts players into rapid improvement.

'I don't know when I last saw Hearts' defence so bad,' wrote the Easter Road centre-forward, who added, 'If their forwards had all been as lively as Jimmy Wardhaugh, it could have been a different result.'

Hearts' luckless goalkeeper that day was Jimmy Watters, Jimmy Brown having been given a free transfer a few months earlier. But Tommy Walker had already made an abortive move to sign the Rangers international, Bobby Brown.

The man who was to become Scotland manager in the 1960s was invited to Tynecastle one Sunday in August for signing talks. Hearts fans awaited the outcome with interest, only to learn 48 hours later that the deal was off for some unstated reason.

That same month, Jimmy Wardhaugh was invited to address the Corstorphine branch of the Supporters' Club and, forthright as ever, told them — 'Hearts fans are the best in the world but the worst when it comes to barracking players.'

He instanced the experience of Tommy Sloan, claiming that the winger had been driven out of Tynecastle by critics. Yet, when Motherwell won the Scottish Cup with Sloan's help, those same critics had demanded to know why Hearts let him leave.

Those who had criticised Jimmy in the past could find no fault with his performances when, as the Trio's fifth anniversary approached, he took over at centre-forward in place of his injured colleague, Willie.

After thrashing three goals past Stirling Albion in a 6-1 win, he and Alfie pooled their scoring skills to beat Dundee 2-1. Suddenly, he found himself in contention for the centre-forward role against Wales, even though Reilly was back playing for Hibs.

But, in Willie's absence, Hearts made a couple of excursions to England which ate into the confidence which they were building up at home. They lost six goals in a floodlit match at Manchester City and seven at West Ham.

Willie duly made his comeback in a less hazardous friendly match at Doncaster which ended 3-1 in Hearts' favour and was reinstated to the League side for their 5-1 win over Raith. He didn't manage a goal that day but Jimmy got three (the first in 18 seconds) and Alfie two.

Jimmy, who finally did lose out to Reilly for a place against Wales, scored another two in a 5-1 win at Hamilton to wedge Hearts into second top position in the League, behind Queen of the South.

All of a sudden the Scottish public took note of Hearts' championship challenge which maintained its momentum in spite of Willie's quick exit from a 3-2 win at Falkirk with knee ligament damage.

Fortunately Willie was back in time for the 4-3 win over Airdrie on January 2, scoring one goal to Jimmy's two as Hearts went to the top of the Division at last, albeit on goal average.

Jim Souness, who had been signed from Hibs, had begun to make an impression by then and he joined Willie, Jimmy and Johnny Urquhart on the scoresheet in a 5-1 win over St Mirren which propelled Hearts into a two-point lead.

Hearts were then better placed to win the League than at any time since the Second World War and they underlined their ambition to do so with a commendable 4-2 win at Dundee, to which Alfie contributed two goals and Willie and Jim Souness one apiece.

Dens Park director, Frank Graham, later described Hearts as a 'team with a title look', adding that he was proud of the show his side had put up against 'the best footballing team in Britain'.

For the record, the forward line that day in January, 1954, was Souness, Conn, Bauld, Wardhaugh and Urquhart. It was to achieve even greater deeds before the year was out . . .

Johnny Urquhart, forward team-mate of the Trio.

Hearts fans rallied to the cause, a crowd of 42,000 being counted for the important 3-2 victory over Celtic at Tynecastle which featured two goals by Willie and a contentious winner in injury time by Jimmy. As the Celtic goalkeeper held a cross ball, Jimmy promptly shoulder-charged him over the line. It was no offence in those days.

The Tynecastle side quickly bundled little Fraserburgh out of the Scottish Cup as they hurried to get on with the business of winning the Championship, and Alfie Conn helped them claim a valuable point against Rangers with an 88th-minute equaliser after Willie and Jimmy had scored in the first half.

Hearts were then seven points ahead of their nearest challengers, Celtic, having played three games more. But, after a sterling Cup win at Queen of the South in which Jimmy scored both their goals, the Tynecastle side slipped to a 4-2 defeat at Raith Rovers.

They were then only five points ahead of Celtic who still had their games in hand, and seemed to be unnerved by a heavy Cup defeat at Aberdeen in which skipper Bobby Parker had the misfortune to fracture his jaw.

League business took them back to Pittodrie the following Saturday but, once more, Hearts were out of luck, finishing as 1-0 losers. Celtic soon moved a point in front and duly claimed their first title in 16 years by beating Hibs 3-0 at Easter Road.

So Hearts had to content themselves with second place, five points behind the Parkhead side who duly completed the double of Scottish Cup and League by beating Aberdeen in the Final at Hampden.

But the despondency soon cleared from Tynecastle as the players, including the young Dave Mackay who had been broken into the first team during the season, took up an invitation to go to South Africa.

It was later claimed that the team spirit which was to fuel so many Hearts successes was fostered on that trip, although that assertion is arguable, for discontent simmered after the directors appeared to renege on a promise to give the players spending money.

Davie Laing, acting captain in the absence through injury of Bobby Parker, assumed the responsibilities of team spokesman and talked his fellow-players out of their collective wish to return home on the understanding that some recompense would be made to them when they returned as scheduled to Tynecastle.

In what appeared to be a vengeful act by the board, Davie was dropped for the start of the new season and prodded into asking for a transfer. Tommy Walker pleaded repeatedly with him to change his mind, but he had a principle to protect and moved to Clyde just when great things were about to happpen at Tynecastle. Hearts had lost a valuable and greatly respected servant and the Trio a good friend.

Davie Laing, an invaluable club servant and good friend of the Trio. Later he was to say, 'A club could spend millions nowadays and not strike as successful a partnership as Alfie, Willie and Jimmy had going.'

'We had all been reared in a super atmosphere at Tynecastle,' he recalled. 'It broke my heart to leave the club and so many good pals including Alfie, Willie and Jimmy. They were always something special.'

CHAPTER FIVE

Success at last

The League Cup had not been kind to Hearts since its inception in 1946 when Scottish football was striving to return to normality after the Second World War. True, they had reached the semi-final at the first try, only to lose 6-2 to Aberdeen at Easter Road. But since then, despite several promising starts, they had been hapless failures in the tournament.

Thus, when they were drawn with Dundee, Falkirk and Celtic in 1954, not even the eternal optimists on the Tynecastle terraces could have imagined that the team's luck would endure anything like as long as it did.

Dundee, whose most inspirational player, Billy Steel, had defected to the USA, were quickly disposed of in a 3-1 win at Tynecastle, Johnny Urquhart, Alfie Conn and Bobby Blackwood scoring the goals.

Unwilling to be upstaged, Jimmy Wardhaugh and Willie Bauld each scored twice in the 6-2 win at Brockville which followed, and Jimmy claimed another goal in the 2-1 victory at Parkhead a few days later.

Only temporarily distracted by a 4-1 defeat at Dens in which Willie headed his third goal of the competition, Hearts proceeded to dismiss Falkirk and Celtic at home by 4-1 and 3-2 respectively, with Willie scoring three times, Alfie and Jimmy once.

Few could have believed that 98 fruitless years might be about to end even after St Johnstone had been beaten on a 7-0 aggregate in the quarter-final in which the Trio contributed an invaluable four goals.

Nor would they have dared predict an historic triumph when Hearts took on Second Division Airdrie in the semi-final at Easter Road, especially when Billy Price put the Broomfield side ahead in the first minute.

'We were high-fliers at the time and really thought we were in with a good chance of getting to the Final of the League Cup that season,' recalled Airdrie's towering teenage centre-half, Doug Baillie, who moved on to Rangers.

'But Hearts ended up taking us apart with a 4-1 win and I ended up in hospital with a dislocated shoulder although the game was well and truly over by the time I suffered the injury trying to prevent the fourth goal.

'Hearts simply knew too much for us. Bobby Parker, who was a hardy sort and coming to the veteran stage, kicked us up and down the park. What a pair of wing-halves Hearts had, too, in Mackay and Cumming. They were as skilful as they were strong.

'Then there were Conn, Bauld and Wardhaugh — brilliant! Bauld was the first player I can remember — Denis Law was the second — who could jump and stay there until the ball came across. His timing was so good, unbelievable really.

'Trying to mark him on the deck was pretty well impossible. How could you mark somebody who just wasn't there? He would drift this way and that. He was never where you wanted him to be.'

So it was that, on the strength of two goals by Jimmy, one each by Willie and Johnny Urquhart, Hearts reached their first Final since losing the Scottish Cup to Celtic in 1907, a year after winning it against Third Lanark.

By way of warming up for Hampden on October 23, Hearts eased to a 2-0 victory at East Fife with goals by Jimmy and Jim Souness, then beat Hibs 2-0 in a floodlit match at Easter Road for which the Trio and Tam Mackenzie were rested. Indeed, the talk was that Jock Adie might take over from Tam in the big game to come but the talk proved unfounded.

Motherwell, of course, were lined up as Hearts' opponents in the Final and Johnny Urquhart recalled that they, like his own team, had enjoyed a reputation for playing 'sheer football' since the pre-war years.

Convincing Scottish Cup winners only two years earlier, they were a potent mix of experience and youth with former Tynecastle players Charlie Cox and Archie Williams in their ranks as well as three young Edinburgh lads, Charlie Aitken, Alex Bain and Jackie Hunter.

Young Bain confessed to modelling his style on that of Willie Bauld, and he was given further, useful instruction by his hero who plundered a hat-trick in Hearts' 4-2 win.

At last, a Cup was on its way to Tynecastle, courtesy also of Jimmy who scored the third goal, although others, including Jim Souness, contributed handsomely to the long-awaited success with sterling performances.

Thousands of disbelieving Hearts fans stood as if cemented into the terraces, chanting, 'We want Bauld', and Jimmy later complained of a headache as a result of the pummelling he had taken from overjoyed supporters on leaving the field.

'The old superstition around Tynecastle was that Hearts would never win a trophy until the tram lines were lifted from Gorgie Road,' Johnny Urquhart recalled, 'but I seem to recall them being lifted about that time, so maybe that helped us!

'It seemed unbelievable that we had won something after almost 50 years and the welcome we got when we drove into Edinburgh was fantastic. Everywhere, there was a mass of bodies, all shouting for the Hearts.'

Pity poor Hibs. They had lost 6-3 to Clyde in Glasgow that same afternoon and had to endure a train journey back to the capital in the company of hundreds of jubilant fans in maroon and white.

For the record, the Hampden teams that memorable October day, six years and two weeks after the Terrible Trio had been united, were:

HEARTS — Duff; Parker, Mackenzie; Mackay, Glidden and Cumming; Souness, Conn, Bauld, Wardhaugh and Urquhart.

MOTHERWELL — Weir; Kilmarnock, McSeveney; Cox, Paton and Redpath; Hunter, Aitken, Bain, Humphries and Williams.

Scorers: Hearts — Bauld (3), Wardhaugh.

Motherwell — Redpath (pen), Bain.

Attendance: 55,640.

At last! Jubilant supporters invade the pitch as Hearts win the Scottish League Cup in 1954. They beat Motherwell 4-2, Willie Bauld scoring a hat-trick.

History was made as Willie fired Hearts into a 2-0 lead with a header, then a shot and, after Willie Redpath had registered a penalty for Motherwell, Jimmy restored his side's two-goal lead with a header immediately before the interval.

Motherwell succeeded in keeping Hearts in check until the final minutes when Willie headed Hearts into a 4-1 lead, and young Bain replied almost instantly with a consolatory second for the Fir Park side.

Naturally, the King claimed most of the headlines, and when he went to share his jubilation with his family in Portobello the following day, a tearful Mrs Bauld senior announced that she was 'the proudest mother in Edinburgh'.

But the critics were mixed in their view of who should share in Willie's adulation. The *Scottish Daily Express* insisted that Alfie had set up the momentous victory by 'engineering the moves which led to the first two goals', while the *Scottish Daily Mail* praised Jimmy for scoring what it deemed to be 'the vital third'.

Chairman Robert Galloway was very proud of all his players, saying, 'Now that we have broken our 48 year hoodoo, we hope that our success will be the forerunner of many others'.

Amongst the many touching telegrams of congratulation which filled Hearts' postbag in the ensuing few days was one from Mrs Davie McLean, widow of the manager whose foresight back in the late 1940s had fashioned the great team of the following decade.

Willie, one of his protégés and Scotland's top scorer for the season so far with 12 goals, confessed, 'No matter how many cups we win in future, nothing will compare in memory with our win over Motherwell. It was like breaking the sound-barrier for the first time, after many heart-breaking failures.'

An unhappy postscript to Hampden was that faithful Jimmy Watters, who had been at Tynecastle for 10 years, many of them as understudy to Jimmy Brown, had lost his place in goal to young Willie Duff after playing in the semi-final against Airdrie. His reluctant response was to ask for a transfer, but Hearts eventually persuaded him to stay on a while.

Two weeks passed before the proud Tynecastle players could display their prize in front of their own fans — the 30,000 who turned out for the home game with Falkirk.

Hearts, who had scored five goals at Stirling Albion on the intervening Saturday, proceeded to do the same again, with Willie and Jimmy both scoring twice and Bobby Parker converting a penalty. They were cheered from first minute to last.

Scotland's selectors were quick to take note of Hearts' growing prowess and sent representatives to assess the form of Willie and Jimmy as well as John Cumming before the eagerly-awaited match with Hungary at Hampden in December.

Paddy Buckley had been the most recent occupant of the centre-forward position but Tommy Muirhead, who had the selectors' ear, reported in the *Express* that Lawrie Reilly was overtaking Willie Bauld in the race to lead Scotland's attack against the celebrated Ferenc Puskas and pals.

'If Reilly wins, it will be because of his grim, persevering determination which Bauld lacks,' Muirhead wrote. 'I saw him against Queen of the South recently and, for the first 20 minutes and last, he was the genius that only Bauld can be. In the 50 minutes in between, he was careless and lethargic.'

In the event, Reilly, who had been out of the Hibs' side for months through illness, regained his international place, although his eternal Edinburgh rival was listed as one of five reserves to travel to Hampden.

Jimmy Wardhaugh and John Cumming enjoyed better luck, surviving a trial played in a mud bath at Falkirk to win their first full caps in a match from which the Scots emerged with great credit, despite their 4-2 defeat.

On the domestic front, Jimmy and the other members of the Trio had continued their good work by hammering in four of the six goals which floored Raith Rovers at Stark Park and, after Willie had claimed two more at Shawfield, Hearts climbed into fourth position in the League.

But the old enemy, inconsistency, attacked their form before the year was out with Rangers winning 4-3 at Tynecastle, in spite of goals by both Willie and Jimmy. Alfie shot two the following week but Hearts stumbled again, dropping a valuable point in a 4-4 draw with Partick Thistle at Firhill.

They resolved to eradicate this flaw in 1955, starting against Hibs in the Ne'erday match at Tynecastle which they won by a spectacular 5-1, their best derby score since the war.

The flood of goals began with one from Alfie in 15 minutes and, in the short spell which followed the interval, Willie swept in two more. Bobby Johnstone promised to stem the tide with a 73rd-minute penalty but it rose rapidly again with further goals by Jim Souness and Jimmy Wardhaugh.

An admiring Jack Harkness duly reported in the *Sunday Post* that 'Hibs were on the receiving end of 10 top-notchers and a genius'. That genius was Willie Bauld who, he added, 'almost lifted Tommy Younger into Gorgie Road' with a first-half shot.

During the big freeze-up that winter, Hearts discussed an invitation to go to the warmer climes of the Argentine as summer tourists, but they shelved the offer in the belief that the SFA might want to take several of their top players abroad at the same time. What price Willie Bauld being among them?

Long since crowned the King of Hearts, he had also been voted the best centre-forward to play for the club in 30 years in a poll conducted by the Tynecastle programme the previous season. For the record the fans' Top Team was: Harkness; Anderson, McClure; Massie, Johnston, Herd; Munro, Walker, Bauld, Black and Murray.

Furthermore, Willie could probably lay claim to being the only player in the country to have a tram stop named after him, for it was said that, when the car pulled up near Tynecastle, the conductor would shout 'Willie Bauld's stop' rather than 'MacLeod Street'.

But the spectre of injury was lurking only a few weeks away as Willie spearheaded Hearts into their Scottish Cup campaign with another resounding Hearts win over Hibs, this time by 5-0, in front of a 45,770 crowd.

He scored twice and Jimmy once in the opening 25 minutes in which Hibs begged for mercy. Jimmy scored again in 66 minutes before Alfie shot the best goal of the match — a 15-yarder which ripped past Willie Miller — some 13 minutes from the end.

Hibs, as the score suggested, were outclassed, reports stating that Dave Mackay and John Cumming shackled Bobby Johnstone and Bobby Combe, whilst the redoubtable Bobby Parker blocked Willie Ormond on the wing.

Hearts were beckoned to Buckie in the next round and routed the Highlanders with a 6-0 win which included a hat-trick for Willie and two goals for his trusty ally, Jimmy.

But then, as Alfie shot two to claim a 2-2 draw in the League at Falkirk, Willie limped off the field with a recurring knee problem which rendered him doubtful for a forthcoming B international with England at Ibrox.

In the event, the fixture was cancelled and Willie passed a fitness test to play against Aberdeen in the third round of the Cup at Tynecastle. He did well, too, equalising Jackie Allister's early goal some fifteen minutes into the second half.

Although Hearts lost the replay 2-1, Willie was fit to face the same opposition in the League the following Saturday and scored both goals in a 2-0 win. Alas, he damaged his knee in a collision with the Aberdeen goalkeeper, Fred Martin, and had to withdraw from the Inter-League game with England at Hampden.

Back he came again, this time to help Hearts consolidate in fourth top position in the League with a goal in a 3-0 win over Clyde. Probably he was grateful not to be playing for Scotland against England at Wembley that same afternoon. They lost by an embarrassing 7-2 with only John Cumming from Hearts among their bedraggled ranks.

Hearts' challenge fizzled out thereafter as they lost to both Rangers and Celtic in the last month of the season, yet contrived to cling to fourth position, which was respectable enough. Willie, like Alfie, missed the final match with a troublesome toe injury.

As a result, he lost the chance to accompany team-mate John Cumming on Scotland's prestigious close-season tour of Yugoslavia, Austria and Hungary. No wonder Hearts fans talked ruefully of the 'Big Tae Disaster'.

In the event, Willie needed treatment for several weeks of the summer break, during which young Davie Mackay was another source of concern. Already an integral part of the Hearts team, the dynamic wing-half had to report to hospital for a belated check on the damage done to one of his ears during the South African trip a year earlier. Worse still, he was due to be called up for National Service.

Three younger lads, Alex Young, George Thomson and Johnny Hamilton, awaited a call-up with a difference — from junior football to Tynecastle. They would help write new chapters in Hearts' colourful tale of the 1950-60s and Alex Young would eventually become a threat to at least one member of the Terrible Trio . . .

CHAPTER SIX

Trio triumphs again

The lingering effects of the 'Big Tae Disaster' stalked Willie Bauld into season 1955-56 although he was fit enough to lay on a goal for Willie Ormond in the Edinburgh Select's 1-1 draw with F.A. Cup winners Newcastle in the annual charity game in August.

By the time that Hearts were mounting their defence of the League Cup in a home tie with Partick Thistle, he was in hospital for further examination of his injury and the precocious Alex Young was in his place in the forward line.

Alex scored a fine, winning goal that day and he followed up quite spectacularly with a hat-trick in a 4-0 victory over East Fife. But Hearts could do no better than qualify for the second phase of the tournament before losing on a punishing 9-5 aggregate to Aberdeen.

Alfie Conn, who scored in the home leg of that tie with the Dons, was deployed at wing-half in place of Davie Mackay when Hearts lost 1-0 at home to Hibs in the League. Willie was still nursing his sore toe and, consequently, missed a 4-1 win at Airdrie in which Jimmy scored two goals.

But Willie was back playing between Alfie and Jimmy — albeit briefly — as Hearts attempted to accelerate their League challenge with a 2-1 win over Celtic in front of a 30,000 Tynecastle crowd.

It was around that time that Jimmy began to get a mention in transfer despatches. Newcastle had reportedly offered a breath-catching £27,000 for his scoring skills and Spurs were reputed to be willing to pay even more.

48

Jimmy, who was about to play for the Scottish League at Sheffield, responded politely to the speculation, saying that he had just moved into a new house in Edinburgh and had a good job in newspapers besides football and was, therefore, happy to remain where he was.

He proceeded to underscore his commitment to Hearts by hitting a hat-trick in a 5-0 win over Stirling Albion, Willie having made an abortive return in a 3-1 defeat at St Mirren the previous week.

Despite scoring Hearts' goal at Love Street, Willie was reported to have played at half-pace and did not re-appear until Hearts' 5-1 victory over Clyde in which Jimmy lashed in four goals and Alfie one. 'Indispensable — that's Bauld', the *Scottish Sunday Express* proclaimed.

Jimmy had also missed the Rangers game in the interim, a fact which may have strengthened Hearts' excuse for losing 4-1 to the Ibrox side whose celebrated centre-half, Willie Woodburn, had been suspended *sine die* by then.

Injury overtook Alfie as Hearts, with Willie and Jimmy back in harness, fired another five goals past Dunfermline with the two surviving Trio members claiming two goals each.

But Alfie was reinstated in time to help the side record their most notable result of the season so far: a 7-1 win over Motherwell in which Willie grabbed another two goals and Jimmy a handsome four.

Hearts were in third place in the League by then, behind Hibs and Celtic. They improved upon that position when they followed up a 2-2 draw at Easter Road, in which Willie and Alfie clawed back a two-goal deficit, with yet another big score: 5-0 against Partick Thistle.

That was an auspicious occasion for the Trio, their 200th appearance together and, by way of a celebration, Alfie scored a hat-trick, leaving Jimmy to put his name to the other two goals.

Statisticians calculated that Conn, Bauld and Wardhaugh had then scored 487 goals between them — 131, 188 and 168 respectively — and the Corstorphine branch of the Supporters' Club agreed that their feat should be recognised with a presentation at their next meeting.

Hearts, having cancelled Jim Souness's contract to allow him to concentrate on business, duly went to the top of the League with a 2-0 win at Dundee, Alfie sharing their goals with Ian Crawford who had been freed by Hibs.

But the Scottish Cup deflected their attention from the Championship and they were pleased to make a promising start in the tournament with a 3-0 win over Forfar in which Alfie slipped through the fog to steal two goals.

Twice in the previous four seasons they had reached the semi-finals of the competition and, with the League Cup triumph still a fresh, inspirational memory, they had confidence enough to believe they could do at least as well this time.

Their optimism was stoked when, with Willie out of hospital after an ankle injury, they thrashed Stirling Albion (as they usually did) by 5-0 in the second round.

Willie began that rout, heading in a typical goal in 13 minutes which moved the *Sunday Express* to record that 'even the snow stopped in the admiration of him'. John Cumming, Alex Young, Alfie and Jimmy struck the additional blows for the Tynecastle team who, because of a clash of colours, played in Rangers' blue.

Hearts had stuttered slightly in the Championship by then, drawing 1-1 at Celtic Park where Alex Young was their scorer, and 2-2 at home with Queen of the South with Alfie and Jimmy getting their goals.

But they recovered well enough to thump four goals past East Fife, despite the absences of Alfie who had a recurring knee injury and Willie who was complaining once more about that now notorious sore toe.

As a result, Alfie missed out on a B international against England at Dundee the following midweek and Hearts had to rush him and Willie to fitness for what was to be a momentous, Scottish Cup quarter-final tie with Rangers at Tynecastle on March 3.

Jimmy Wardhaugh walked briskly to his nearest barber's shop on the morning of the game. He had had his hair cut before the Forfar tie and, again, before the one with Stirling Albion, and was beginning to believe it a lucky omen!

In the event, his recently-acquired superstition was reinforced

Ian Crawford, freed by Hibs, was to join in the scoring with the Trio.

when Hearts proceeded to beat Rangers for the first time in the tournament for 61 years by the resounding score of 4-0.

Harry Andrew reported in the *Sunday Express* that this long-overdue success was effectively sealed in the 30-second spell during the first half in which Ian Crawford and Willie gave Hearts a two-goal lead. The Tynecastle side stepped out then on a victory march which, the writer recorded, was 'majestic, certain, adorned by all that is best in football artistry'.

Crawford's opening goal, a header in 36 minutes, broke a sustained period of Rangers' pressure and irked the gigantic Ibrox captain, George Young. Blatantly risking a penalty, he used both hands in an attempt to stop the ball crossing the line, but failed.

Whilst he and his team-mates were still debating the loss of that goal, Alfie slipped the ball through to Willie who, drawing George Niven off his line, calmly prodded Hearts into what proved to be an unassailable lead.

Alfie followed up with a stinging third goal, shot from the edge of the box — one of his 'specials' — in the 63rd minute and Willie combined with both him and Jimmy to knock in the fourth some 10 minutes later.

The *Sunday Post's* Jack Harkness shared colleague Harry Andrew's opinion that Alfie was the outstanding player in that outstanding match, enthusing, 'He surely has no superior at inside-right in Scotland today.' Slowly, some Scottish selectors were coming round to that view, too.

Amazingly, the man with one of the hardest shots in the game had collected only a couple of League caps by then, although he was given almost instant hope of winning a full cap when he was chosen to play against South Africa at Ibrox in what was effectively a trial for the England game the following month.

Scotland won 2-1 with goals by Lawrie Reilly and Bobby Collins but, alas, Alfie was forced to withdraw because of an ankle injury. His place went to Ian McMillan of Airdrie who duly deputised for the injured Collins against the English at Hampden.

Willie Bauld could sympathise with Alfie. Only too well did he know the despair of having to withdraw from a Scotland side for, despite persistent rumours to the contrary, Willie was proud to represent his country.

Alfie's consolation was that he was fit for the Cup semi-final against Raith Rovers at Easter Road, Hearts having drawn 1-1 with Rangers in a League match by then and stayed in their slipstream in the surge towards the title.

Alfie: 'He surely has no superior at inside-right in Scotland today.'

But Alfie ran into further misfortune in the goalless draw with the Kirkcaldy side whose international centre-half, Willie McNaught, contrived to blot out Willie Bauld as few others could have done.

Within minutes of being thwarted by a brilliant save by the Raith goalkeeper, Alfie was denied a penalty when he was bowled over in the Fife side's box. Adding to his anguish was the fact that he dislocated his shoulder in that incident and left the ground with his arm in a sling.

On top of the frustrating result, this was drastic luck for Alfie and Hearts but what else should they have expected? Jimmy Wardhaugh had taunted Fate by forgetting to get his hair cut!

So Alfie, whose two goals against Forfar had set Hearts off on their Cup run, was forced to sit out the replay, Alex Young moving into his position to accommodate young Johnny Hamilton on the right wing.

Wee Hammy responded by helping set up goals for Jimmy and Ian Crawford after the former had given Hearts an early lead and Tam Mackenzie had denied Raith an equaliser by scrambling a shot off the line.

A crowd of 54,000 — 4,000 fewer than on the Saturday — applauded that 3-0 victory for the Tynecastle team who, commendably, had now gone all the way to Hampden without losing a goal. But what price Hearts to win the Final against Celtic whose record in the tournament was intimidating? And what chance had Alfie of being fit to help them?

Both he and Willie Bauld were missing from the side which reverted to League business and beat Dunfermline by 5-0, Davie Mackay highlighting their performance with two goals.

The Cup Final was only three weeks away by then and, while Alfie made a tentative comeback in a 4-1 defeat at Aberdeen, Willie was still an absentee — and so was Jimmy.

But Hearts, who had virtually settled for third place in the League by then, did not have the monopoly on injury problems. Across in Glasgow, Celtic were concerned about the condition of a certain Jock Stein who had developed a painful and worrying growth on his ankle. Bobby Collins, Celtic's tiny terrier of an inside-forward, soon joined him on the sidelines.

A week before the Final, Hampden played host to Scotland versus England, a match which ended in a 1-1 draw, although Alec Young, one of Alfie Conn's champions, insisted in the *Scottish Daily Mail* that a better result would have been realised if the Tynecastle forward had been playing.

Alfie went some way to confirming the point 48 hours later by thrashing a hat-trick in Hearts' astonishing 8-3 win over Falkirk at Tynecastle. Jimmy twice put his name on the scoresheet that day and Willie once, albeit three minutes from time with the crowd willing him to get a goal.

Simultaneously, Celtic were drawing 2-2 in a friendly match with Manchester United, their injury problems being compounded on that occasion when goalkeeper Dick Beattie had to be led off the field after a clash in his penalty box.

Yet, despite the portents, the all-knowing bookmakers still installed Celtic as favourites to win the Cup, pricing them at 5/4 against and Hearts 6/4. Bobby Evans, the Parkhead captain, appeared to underwrite the odds when he insisted, 'So long as we have 11 men in Celtic jerseys on the field, we will be in with a shout. Never mind how many goals Hearts scored on Monday. Saturday will be different.'

Old favourite, Johnny Urquhart, was on the verge of joining his home-town team, Raith Rovers, as Hearts' big day drew nearer. Davie Mackay, serving with the Army in England, responded to the bugle call from Tynecastle and travelled north in the company of fellow-soldier and forthcoming Hampden opponent, Eric Smith, of Celtic. Ian Crawford, stationed in Inverness, travelled south.

Come the morning of Saturday, April 21, Hearts sought to summon all the good fortune they could. Jimmy Wardhaugh made sure that he went for his lucky haircut and groundsman Matt Chalmers rushed through to Glasgow to book the favoured home dressing room.

Then, as the team sped west by train, each man wearing a sprig of white heather in his buttonhole, Alfie inadvertently spilled his cup of tea and, according to Freddie Glidden, it stained a heart shape in the tablecloth.

'We regarded this as another good omen,' recalled Freddie who had taken over as captain after the luckless Bobby Parker had had to undergo a cartilage operation before a ball was kicked in the Scottish Cup that season. Unlike nowadays, the rehabilitation period after such surgery was lengthy.

Bobby had to reserve his best form for the dressing room where, in a hilarious attempt to untangle his team-mates' nerves before kick-off, he reportedly appeared in a grass skirt. What a picture! Joining in the fun, groundsman Chalmers made his entry wearing a frock-coat, fashionable around 1906 when Hearts had last won the trophy.

The final whistle blows. Hearts have beaten Celtic 3-1 in the 1956 Cup Final. Willie Bauld jumps into the arms of injured skipper Bobby Parker who has dashed onto the pitch. Alfie Conn throws his arms round trainer Harvey.

The following teams then filed out on the Hampden field, the deafening roar of a 132,840 crowd threatening to burst their eardrums:

CELTIC — Beattie; Meechan, Fallon; Smith, Evans and Peacock; Craig, Haughney, Mochan, Fernie and Tully.

HEARTS — Duff; Kirk, Mackenzie; Mackay, Glidden and Cumming; Young, Conn, Bauld, Wardhaugh and Crawford.

A tentative start by Hearts soon gave way to some cunning play by the Trio, Willie Bauld drifting from one side of the field to the other in an attempt to shake off the attentions of Bobby Evans.

Alfie and Jimmy combined then for the latter to deceive Celtic's Frank Meechan with a perfect pass to Ian Crawford whose shot bounced to safety off the feet of Dick Beattie who had been pronounced fit on the morning of the match.

Another shot of the final scene. For Hearts, jubilation. For Celtic, dejection.

Sensing Celtic's apprehension, the Trio set up another dangerous move which led to Alfie serving the soldier on Hearts' left wing. From the edge of the penalty box, Private Crawford of the Cameron Highlanders thrashed the first goal past the helpless Beattie.

Celtic pushed back strongly and even Willie was spied in his own penalty area on occasions before Jimmy set up a chance which was squandered uncharacteristically by Alex Young who, unknown to his team-mates, had been unwell for several days beforehand.

If the football was not of the highest order, the excitement tingled the nerves of the huge crowd as Jimmy let fly with a terrific drive which Evans headed over his own cross-bar and Alfie fired in the fierce free-kick which was just too high.

Thereabouts, John Cumming clashed accidentally with Willie Fernie and had to be led off the field with blood weeping from a wound above his eye. He was advised during the interval that he could play on so long as he moved to the left wing and did not attempt to head the ball.

But, ignoring instructions, the courageous Cumming was back at his battle-station in midfield, a sponge held to his brow, when

Later . . . Willie Bauld drinks from the Cup.

Willie Bauld eluded Evans to deliver a 49th-minute cross to Alex Young who, in turn, invited Ian Crawford to hook in a second goal.

A gift of a goal six minutes later allowed Celtic to snatch some of the initiative back from their Edinburgh opponents, Mike Haughney having barged into Willie Duff to prod the loose ball over the line.

Boldly, the Parkhead side pressed for an equaliser, bravely Freddie Glidden and company denied them one. Then, with nine minutes remaining, Willie re-directed a free-kick into the path of Alfie who blasted Hearts' third and final goal in their historic, 3-1 triumph.

Wellwishers flooded into Hearts' lucky home dressing room afterwards, the most prominent of them being their patron, Lord Rosebery. Then Celtic manager Jimmy McGrory and chairman Bob Kelly came in to congratulate Tommy Walker and his tearful players.

Proud Edinburgh prepared to welcome back her conquering heroes for the second time in less than two years and another

A happy postscript to that Cup Final win was that Alfie was awarded his first full cap, scoring for Scotland in their 1-1 draw with Austria at Hampden in May.

great celebration was signalled as Freddie Glidden held the Cup aloft on the open-topped bus which carried him and his team-mates to their victory dinner in the West End.

It was another unforgettable episode in the Trio's epic tale and nobody really cared that the winning team were on the end of a 1-0 defeat at Motherwell a couple of days later as they caught up with their backlog of League games.

Tam Mackenzie spoke for his team-mates when he enthused, 'We've won the League Cup and now the Scottish Cup. Next season it will be the Championship.' As the best team in the country and, arguably, the best team Scotland had produced since the war, they were entitled to believe it.

Two happy Hampden postscripts were that Ian Crawford was picked to play for the British Army against the French, with the great Duncan Edwards of Manchester United stationed at his shoulder, while fellow goalscorer Alfie was awarded that elusive first full cap, against Austria at Hampden on May 2.

Aged 29 and in his prime, Alfie scored the Scots' goal in a 1-1 draw, sidestepping an opponent in the 10th minute and lashing in a left-foot shot from 25 yards' range. This was oh-so typical of him and the *Scottish Daily Mail* reported, 'He was the only success in an attack which failed. He worked like a hero and his goal was a beauty.'

Such praise again posed the question of why the Scottish selectors had waited so long to acknowledge Alfie's talents. But, then again, hadn't they also been much too miserly in their recognition of Willie's and Jimmy's?

CHAPTER SEVEN

A Tilt at the Title

Tam Mackenzie had laid down the challenge to Hearts by identifying their next target as being the Championship, and the Trio, not to mention such steely competitors as Davie Mackay, Fred Glidden and John Cumming, seemed ready to pick it up.

Rich in skill and strength, the Tynecastle team which prepared for season 1956-57 was also ambitious and willed on by a fervent, though sometimes fickle, support.

If only Hearts could avoid serious injuries, they might just be

The Hearts line-up for season 1956-57. Back row, l-r: Howieson, Kirk, J. Thomson, Murray, Brown, G. McKay, Bauld and Cumming. Middle row, l-r: Neilson, D. McKay, Kidd, Milne, Pagan, McKenzie, Foley, Parker and Findlay. Front row, l-r: Young, Bowman, Conn, G. Campbell, Glidden, R. Campbell, Wardhaugh, G. Thomson and Hamilton.

good and consistent enough to fend off the Old Firm and other rivals like Hibs and Aberdeen and take the title for the first time in the twentieth century.

But, recognising Willie Bauld's bad luck especially, they knew that they could not count on Fortune doing them any favours. As the Hearts programme was to lament, Willie's injuries ranged from 'rib to toe', and while Jimmy, at least, was better blessed, Alfie possibly wasn't.

Having made his mark at last with Scotland, scoring in his debut against Austria, he had the painful misfortune to break his jaw only a few months later and could not be considered for the subsequent internationals against Wales, Northern Ireland and Yugoslavia.

It was in a 3-2 win at Easter Road that Alfie suffered the injury which was to put him out of the side until January 1957. Yet, to their huge credit, Hearts were able to reach the top of the League in his lengthy absence and give the impression that they intended to stay there . . .

The aforementioned derby win, in which Jimmy scored twice, propelled them to a flying start in the campaign although it was hardly as spectacular as the result with which they began the season.

In their opening League Cup tie at Tynecastle, they beat their city rivals by 6-1, Jimmy claiming two goals, and Bobby Kirk converting two penalties and missing a third. This, after Eddie Turnbull had given Hibs an early lead.

Jackie Wren made his first appearance in the Hibs' goal that day and another debutant was old friend, Davie Laing, who had returned to Edinburgh to play with the capital's other team after his spell with Clyde.

'John Paterson was injured and we had to re-shuffle our team at half-time with me ending up at left-back,' Davie recalled. His seemed a reasonable excuse for such a result although Hearts contrived to win the return match also, by 2-1, with goals by Jimmy and Alex Young.

Jimmy, who struck a hat-trick in a 5-0 win over Falkirk in the League Cup, was soon to join Willie in the Scottish League side which thrashed seven goals past the Irish League in Belfast.

Jimmy Wardhaugh turns out for Scotland against Northern Ireland in November 1956.

Jimmy's tally on that occasion was two goals while Willie's was three.

According to Jack Harkness, it was the 'first time that Willie Bauld had shown his Hearts class in a Scotland jersey' but, because of the now predictable injuries, Willie did not get much chance to display that class again, even at club level, until late on in 1956.

D

Against East Fife in a League match at Tynecastle, though, he scored twice yet Hearts lost 5-2. Poor Jimmy suffered the brunt of the fans' frustration in defeat, despite having scored 12 goals by that point of the season and 34 the previous term.

Jimmy's consolation was that he was chosen to play for Scotland against Northern Ireland at Hampden in November, an honour he accepted gratefully although he was known to be fourth choice for the inside-left position.

Having scored once against the League of Ireland at Shawfield that year, as well as twice against the Irish League in Belfast, Jimmy should not have been short of confidence for his Home International debut.

The *Scottish Daily Mail* described him in its match preview as 'one of the best ball-playing inside-forwards in the country who should link well with Jackie Mudie and Lawrie Reilly'.

(Intriguingly, Reilly was reported to have received a letter before that match offering him £150 to call off. From a Willie Bauld fan, perhaps?)

But in the wake of Scotland's 1-0 win, the same journal expressed 'nothing but sympathy' for the Tynecastle player who worked at least as hard as he ever did for Hearts without getting a break in front of goal.

'Wardhaugh had to do a double job, left-half Doug Cowie of Dundee having been carried off with an ankle injury in 22 minutes,' the report added. 'It was like a hoodoo because a similar thing happened when he played against Hungary, too.'

Alas, Jimmy was never to play for the full Scotland team again — a fact which prompted clubmate John Cumming to reflect, 'There wasn't a finer inside-forward in the game than him yet, at international level, he seemed to be all burnt up, as if he couldn't relax.'

By the time that Jimmy had played against Northern Ireland, Alfie was still nursing his broken jaw and still feeding from an invalid cup. But Hearts had gone to the top of the League with Willie's winning goal against Partick Thistle and they had every intention of staying there.

New players were being introduced in emergencies: Jim McFadzean in the forward line, Andy Bowman at half-back and

Gordon Marshall in goal. Still, Hearts kept on winning, a 6-1 victory over Queen's Park being one of the most spectacular before the turn of the year.

Jimmy contented himself with one goal in that high-scoring game, Ian Crawford and Jimmy Murray claiming two each. Then Jimmy scored against Celtic at Parkhead to register a vital point for the Tynecastle team.

It seemed to matter little to Hearts' League hopes that they lost 5-3 in a mid-December mudbath at Ibrox in which Jimmy scored twice and the fit-again Willie Bauld once.

Hearts still finished the year in top position, five points ahead of Motherwell who had played a match less and seven points in front of Rangers who treasured two games in hand.

Nor did Hearts seem to be unnerved by the fact that they began 1957 with a rare home defeat by Hibs. Still without Alfie and with Willie back on the sidelines, they recovered their momentum by beating Dundee 3-0.

Alfie came back at last in a 3-1 win at East Fife, a game in which Willie laid on a fine goal for Jimmy. The King, though barely fit, was then being mentioned as a rival to Lawrie Reilly for the centre-forward role against England at Wembley.

He and Jimmy were duly selected to play for the Scotland B team to face England B at Birmingham but neither emerged from a disappointing defeat there with a realistic hope of playing at Wembley. And, of course, they did not.

Hearts had temporarily suspended their League challenge in order to make their first defence of the Scottish Cup, against Rangers at Tynecastle in front of a 47,000 crowd.

The home fans among them hoped for a repeat of the previous season's Cup result against the Glasgow side. Instead, they had to suffer the reverse with Rangers winning this time by 4-0, in spite of the fact that Hearts showed only one team change, Wilson Brown for Willie Duff in goal.

Hearts looked good only until the 20th minute when Alex Young missed a chance set up for him by Alfie. Ten minutes later, they were 3-0 down with Johnny Hubbard having sparked Rangers' scoring burst with one of his expertly-taken penalties.

Those occasionally fickle Tynecastle fans promptly called for the heads of Willie and Alfie although the defeat, painful as it was, happened to be Hearts' first in six weeks.

Whether influenced or not by the criticism of two of his most esteemed three players, Tommy Walker left both out of the subsequent League match, against Airdrie, which resulted in a 2-0 win. Jimmy Wardhaugh, the Trio's survivor, was edged off the scoresheet that day in February by Alex Young and Jimmy Murray although he was then joint top scorer in Scotland, with 26 goals.

Willie was reinstated for a 1-1 draw with Falkirk in which Jimmy Murray, Alfie's deputy, scored for Hearts. Then, without both Alfie and Jimmy, Hearts were held 2-2 at Firhill with Willie scoring the first of their second-half goals.

Jimmy was reportedly in a depression the following week and asked to be left out of the side to face Raith Rovers at Tynecastle. But, selected at the last minute, he and Willie scored in the 2-1 win which helped restore the team's balance at the top of the table.

It was reported thereabouts, some 11 months after Hearts had won the Scottish Cup, that their name had not yet been inscribed on either the trophy or its base. Apparently, there was no room left to record their long-awaited triumph of 1956 and the SFA were still awaiting delivery of a new plinth.

Hearts, however, had lost interest in the trophy that season and it was their Cup conquerors, Rangers, who were beginning to threaten their chance of taking the title. Although seven points behind in mid-March, the Ibrox side had three games in hand.

Two goals by Willie helped Hearts kick ahead again with a 3-1 win over Celtic at Tynecastle, this in the week that he learned he had been overlooked for Scotland's Wembley team. And, on the day that his rival Reilly, who was less than fit, played in a 2-1 defeat by the English, Hearts recorded an important 3-1 win at Motherwell with Alfie getting one of their goals.

Reilly, it transpired, had accidentally injured his foot before the match and a section of the Press demanded to know why Willie had not been flown down to London to replace him!

Hearts then faced a crucial and potentially decisive League match against Rangers at Tynecastle but they lost it by 1-0 to allow the Ibrox side to move to within two points of them with two games fewer played. Had their nerves begun to shred?

Maybe not, for they proceeded to beat Queen of the South 2-0 away with goals by Willie and Jimmy and Aberdeen 3-0 at Tynecastle with Jimmy scoring twice. But Rangers were now ahead on goal average with a game still to play and, to Hearts' chagrin, they duly claimed the title by two points.

So Tam Mackenzie had been a shade too optimistic when, after the Scottish Cup victory a year earlier, he had declared, 'Now for the Championship.' Yet, what poor luck Hearts had had with injuries, the Trio managing to play only three matches together during the campaign. John Cumming and Freddie Glidden had also had to endure anguished spells on the sidelines which did not help the balance of the side.

Encouragingly, however, Hearts had finished the last three seasons in fourth, third and second places respectively. Could they continue the sequence at the next attempt? The question provided the big talking point of the summer — not a sunny one for Willie Bauld, as it turned out.

He had limped out of season 1956-57 with a recurrence of his ankle injury and, as a result, was denied the chance to face Spain in a World Cup qualifying tie at Hampden in May. Was there no end to the man's ill-fortune?

A happier man that month was young Dave Mackay who was picked to make his international debut in the return game with the Spaniards in Madrid. Some years earlier, when Davie had played zestfully in a youth game at Tynecastle, Willie had prophesied, 'Hearts might start to win things when that lad is in the team.'

By 1957, it could be seen that time had invested truth in Willie's forecast, the League Cup and the Scottish Cup already having been won, with Mackay's competitive urge, like that of John Cumming, providing ample support for the Trio's talents.

But the most glittering prize, the League Championship, still eluded Hearts. It had done so for 60 years. Willie was now 29, a year older than Jimmy and a year younger than Alfie. The Trio were not going to have many more chances to complete their set of medals.

CHAPTER EIGHT

Jimmy grabs the Glory

Tommy Walker spent much of the summer of '57 wondering how to put an extra layer of polish on a side which had been glittering for several years. It didn't threaten to be a difficult task as they sparkled in a 9-2 League Cup win over Queens Park in which the Trio shared six goals, three for Jimmy Wardhaugh and two for Willie Bauld.

Yet, for the second successive season, Hearts failed to qualify for the later stages of the tournament. Only when they launched into their League campaign with a 6-0 win over Dundee at Tynecastle did the manager again begin to spot signs of the brightness which was to dazzle many opponents in the months to come.

Willie was quick to follow the scoring lead of Jimmy Murray that day against Dundee. Then Ian Crawford, with two goals, Bobby Kirk with a penalty, and Jimmy, who had been slow to re-sign during the close-season, all joined the spree.

Their good fortune was not shared by Alfie who was hirpling on a damaged ankle by then and destined, for the second successive season, not to re-appear until after the turn of the year. In his absence, Hearts followed up the destruction of Dundee by annihilating Airdrie 7-2 at Broomfield, Jimmy celebrating what was to prove the first of three hat-tricks in the League.

Willie's fine form was not rewarded with a goal against the Lanarkshire side although he was reported to have given Doug Baillie a rather uncomfortable afternoon. But, after Jimmy had scored a quickie in the 3-1 home win over Hibs, Willie was back

Jimmy, ready for another of
his non-stop performances.

on standard with two goals to Jimmy's three in a 9-0 trouncing of
East Fife.

That was Hearts' fourth match of the Championship and they
had already scored 25 goals, an astonishing statistic. It was the
kind of eye-opening form which was to sweep Willie into the
Scottish League side for whom he scored once against the League
of Ireland and twice against the Irish League.

It was the kind of form, too, which was to put him in line for a
place in the full Scotland team to play in the World Cup qualifier
against Switzerland. But, in the event, Jackie Mudie held on to
the centre-forward position and Willie's luck was soon on the
slide.

Mind you, he was on hand to share with Jimmy and Alex
Young the three goals which marked a splendid, 3-2 fightback by

Hearts at Ibrox and, again, to register their 50th League goal of the season, in a 2-1 defeat by Clyde at Shawfield. Jimmy then had to carry the Trio's torch for many weeks to come.

It was reported around that time that Willie had a groin strain although the fine form of Alex Young had at least as much to do with his sudden demise after Shawfield. When Hearts duly thrashed Falkirk by 9-1, only a couple of weeks after firing eight goals past Queens Park, it was evident that Alex was the pretender to the King's throne.

Young, in fact, scored four of the nine goals against Falkirk, having bagged three of the eight against Queen's. Jimmy, eager to stay in the scoring frame, contented himself with a single here and there although he did manage to score twice at Raith Rovers in early December.

Jack Harkness lamented in the *Sunday Post* that the Trio had not played as a unit since the end of August, but many Hearts fans had probably not noticed. A new Trio of Murray, Young and Wardhaugh had evolved and, judged by their scoring deeds, it was hard to tell the difference.

These high-scoring Hearts had surged to the top of the League from the start, only to be overtaken for the briefest of periods by their city rivals, Hibs, who had played a game more.

By the end of the year, when Jimmy and Alex Young claimed a 2-0 win over Celtic at Parkhead, Hearts had taken on the look of champions elect with no fewer than 71 goals in 17 matches. Welcoming the arrival of a new and potentially momentous year with a 2-0 win at Easter Road, Hearts then destroyed Dundee for the second time in the season, Jimmy bagging his third hat-trick in their 5-0 win.

All of Scotland had begun to applaud the Tynecastle team and the new Trio of Jimmy Murray, Alex Young and Jimmy Wardhaugh, as well as Dave Mackay, were being tipped to go with Scotland to the 1958 World Cup Finals.

Lesser men than Alfie Conn and Willie Bauld may have envied their success although Alfie at least was reinstated, in place of the injured Jimmy, for the 7-2 victory over Third Lanark. He was credited with making a good and eager comeback, his shooting power being as obvious as it had been before although a goal eluded him that day.

Jimmy Murray, in the absence of Conn and Bauld, was to make up a new Trio with Jimmy Wardhaugh and Alex Young.

Rival clubs were now making discreet enquiries about the availability of Willie Bauld who still stood on the sidelines, patiently awaiting the chance to add to the 10 League and League Cup goals he had claimed before his eclipse in November. But Tommy Walker weighed sentiment against good sense and persisted with Alex Young.

At least Willie could reflect on having scored that historic 50th

League goal of the season and he could not begrudge his old ally Alfie the honour of scoring the 100th in a 4-0 win against Motherwell at Fir Park in February, 1958.

Playing only his second match since August, Alfie started the scoring that historic day with a 48th-minute header which the Motherwell goalkeeper, Hastie Weir, mistakenly thought would drop past the post. Jimmy Milne, with a penalty, and Jimmy Murray punished him with two additional goals before Alfie completed Hearts' century with a strong shot in the final minutes.

It had taken Hearts a mere 24 matches to knock up the hundred. Only Motherwell, back in the 1930s, had scored at such a prolific rate and their record of 119 League goals was the Tynecastle team's next target.

But, first, they had a Scottish Cup tie against Hibs to attend to.

Victories over East Fife and Albion Rovers had set them in opposition to their Edinburgh rivals in the third round at Tynecastle. Given that Hearts had won the two League derbies by that stage in the season, they may have assumed that they would win the third without too much trouble. In the event, they scored three goals, Jimmy Wardhaugh putting his name to one of them, but a certain Joe Baker scored Hibs' four and Hearts were out of the tournament for another year.

'We didn't beat Hearts nearly as often as we might have done in those days, even though we tended to go into most of the derby matches as favourites,' recalled the formidable Eddie Turnbull of Hibs who, that particular season, ended a six-year exile from international football to go to the World Cup in Sweden.

Then, looking back to the time when Conn, Bauld and Wardhaugh were without rivals for their places in the Tynecastle forward line, Eddie added, 'They developed a fantastic understanding. Alfie was a good, strong and hard-working player who scored a lot of goals. Jimmy was a contrast, a ball-playing type who also had a high scoring rate, as the record shows.

'Then there was Willie. In my book, he was supreme, a super player. Unlike our own Lawrie Reilly who was sharp as a tack and never stopped moving, Willie was more the play-making type who led his line well. Brilliant in the air, of course, and, again, a fine goal-scorer.'

Apparently unhurt by that Cup defeat, Hearts resumed their most promising League challenge since 1897 with Alfie, playing in place of Jimmy, sending them in pursuit of a new scoring record by claiming two goals in a 4-1 win against Queens Park.

By way of reflecting the disciplinary difference between then and now, it is worth recording that the booking which Alex Young sustained that day at Hampden was Hearts' first of the season.

Hearts then faced a run-in of nine matches from which, theoretically, they needed 14 points to win their first Championship in 61 years. Would they falter as before? The answer was an emphatic 'No', as they stretched their sequence of victories through to the end of March when they beat Raith Rovers 4-1 at Tynecastle.

That was another historic day, the one on which Jimmy Murray equalled Motherwell's record of 119 goals in a season only three minutes after kick-off, and Jimmy Wardhaugh smashed it just four minutes later, with a crafty header from a cross by Bobby Blackwood.

'The ball just seemed to float over and I had the whole wide goal to pop it into,' a jubilant Jimmy enthused afterwards.

By the time that Jimmy Murray and Alex Young had surged through the mud to score again, Hearts had set a staggering new standard of 122 goals in 30 games. Alas, a crowd of only 9,000 was there to applaud them, the less hardy having stayed at home out of the lashing rain.

Hearts had also amassed 55 points and could have declared themselves champions at Rugby Park the following week had young George Thomson, an otherwise impressive fixture in the team by then, avoided the misfortune of scoring through his own goal to cancel Andy Bowman's effort in a 1-1 draw.

Dave Mackay was out of the team by that point, having broken a bone in his foot at Falkirk. But Hearts' momentum was harder to break and, with time acting as their ally, they celebrated their long-awaited and tearful title success at Paisley where Jimmy Wardhaugh had the honour of scoring in their momentous victory.

Mind you, it was a close enough result at 3-2 in Hearts' favour.

Alex Young gave them the lead in seven minutes, St Mirren equalised in 58. Then Jimmy scored two minutes later only to see the value of his effort wiped out shortly afterwards. Eventually, it was Alex Young who put the issue beyond doubt — but what an issue!

Champions at last! Cheered through their two remaining matches, both of them ending in victory, Hearts finished with an amazing total of 132 goals to their credit as well as 62 points, 13 more than their nearest challengers, Rangers, and exactly double the number collected by Hibs.

No player was more deserving of his medal than Jimmy Wardhaugh whose haul of 28 goals in 30 League appearances made him the very model of consistency. Jimmy Murray, with 27 goals in 33 appearances, was confirmed as a World Cup player and accompanied the Scotland squad to Sweden where he played in two of their three matches.

Ever-present Alex Young's claim to joining him was overlooked, despite his 24 goals, although Dave Mackay was fit enough to make the trip to Scandinavia and play in the Scots' last game.

But what of Alfie Conn and Willie Bauld on whose behalf Hearts had to seek Scottish League permission to strike replica medals? Alfie had featured in only five of Hearts' 34 League games and scored four goals while Willie had appeared in just nine for a reward of five goals, the last of them coming in the only defeat, way back in November at Shawfield.

Upstaged by Jimmy Murray and Alex Young, they seemed to have played their last starring roles for the Tynecastle team. Yet it was only a matter of weeks before Willie was back on centre stage as Hearts brought various houses down on their close-season tour of North America.

Jack Harkness wrote during that summer that he had leafed through Canadian newspapers and read coast-to-coast headlines in praise of Willie's form. This man cannot be finished, he asserted. Willie responded by pointing out that the opposition had not been very powerful but he was always modest about his own talents.

Whatever the case, Hearts in general and Willie in particular carried a splendid impression over the Atlantic that year. George Anderson, secretary of the Canadian Football Association, was reported as saying, 'Hearts had a wonderful tour, they were a wonderful team and great ambassadors for Scotland. I'm sorry that Scotland did not do too well in the World Cup but with the cream of the talent here in Canada . . .'

CHAPTER NINE

Trio Minus One

Half a century's aspirations had been fulfilled within the space of four marvellous years, Hearts having won the League Cup, the Scottish Cup and the Championship since 1954. They could do worse than strive to win them all again although nobody would have given an old tanner for their chances of reclaiming the League Cup when they began their challenge in 1958 with a 3-0 defeat by Rangers at Ibrox.

It was a match in which only Jimmy Wardhaugh represented the Terrible Trio, Alfie and Willie being deployed with the reserves in a 1-1 draw at Tynecastle. But Willie celebrated his recall to the first team in the succeeding tie against Third Lanark at Tynecastle, joining Jimmy and Johnny Hamilton on the scoring list in a 3-0 victory.

The King was to enjoy even greater success against the same opponents a couple of weeks later but, in the meantime, he helped Hearts gain revenge over Rangers by scoring the first of their goals in a 2-1 win at Tynecastle.

It was a match almost totally distorted by injuries, Jimmy Wardhaugh reverting from inside-forward to centre-half to allow the injured Jimmy Milne to limp on the left wing after Willie had given Hearts the lead in 46 minutes.

Jimmy was stricken by misfortune almost immediately he had taken on his new role, conceding a penalty with which the peerless Johnny Hubbard equalised.

Rangers' goalkeeper, Norrie Martin, was injured then and

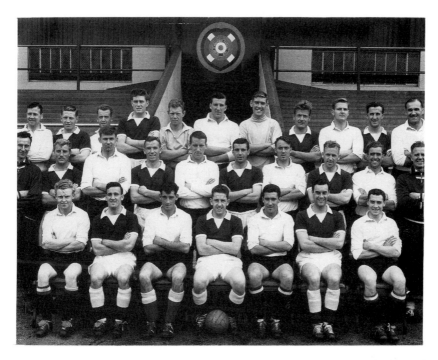

The Hearts line-up for season 1958-59. Back row, l-r: Conn, Blackwood, Lough, Glover, Brown, Robertson, Marshall, Bauld, Higgins, Wardhaugh, McKenzie. Middle row, l-r: D. McLeod (Assistant Trainer), Bowman, McFadzean, Cumming, Smith, Thomson, McIntosh, Kirk, Lindores, J. Harvey (Trainer). Front row, l-r: Goldie, Hamilton, Fraser, Mackay, Crawford, Murray, Paton.

Bobby Shearer took over from him before he, too, took a knock but elected to play on in the still-traditional yellow jersey. Only a minute remained when Jimmy Milne, the first casualty, scored the winner.

The aforementioned return match with Third Lanark was next on Hearts' schedule and they came through it in some style, winning 5-4 with Willie registering a superb hat-trick. Even the Thirds fans applauded Hearts' centre-forward at full-time, which pleased him no end.

A subsequent victory over Raith Rovers assured Hearts of a place in the later stages of the tournament for the first time in three years but a more prestigious competition demanded their attention, albeit briefly.

Drawn away from home to Standard Liège in the first round of the European Cup, the Scottish champions lost by an embarrassing 5-2. The prospect of having to score at least four goals in the home leg haunted Hearts who, in the event, managed only two in a 2-1 win.

Willie, badly bruised that night during a painful encounter with the Belgian centre-half, claimed the distinction of scoring both Hearts' goals but he was hardly consoled, saying, 'Despite the fact that it was our first competitive occasion in Europe, we should have done better.'

Hearts had made a flying start to the League by then, beating Hibs by 4-0 at Easter Road before resuming in the League Cup with an aggregate 8-2, quarter-final win over Ayr United in which Willie contented himself with just one goal.

They followed up with a battling 4-3 win over Airdrie, in which Willie scored a 72nd-minute winner with a brave, diving header from Jimmy's cross, to move again into early, pole position in the championship race.

But while Willie's star had risen once more at Tynecastle, Alfie Conn's was fading from view and in the last week of September, almost exactly 10 years after the Trio's triumphant formation, he was sold to Raith Rovers for £3,000.

Only a few days short of his 32nd birthday, Alfie could not and did not complain about his way-going. He had had the honour of serving Hearts during the most distinguished spell in their history and had etched his name indelibly in the Tynecastle legend as a member of the Terrible Trio.

His proud record revealed that he had scored 219 goals in 14 years and, if his injury-scarred legs were not quite so strong as they had been, he went to Starks Park in the certain knowledge that he would score a few more.

Ironically, though, Alfie had to miss out on a debut against old Edinburgh rivals, Hibs, because of flu, and as he lay shivering in his bed on Saturday, September 27, old pal Willie fired five goals past poor old Third Lanark in an 8-3 win at Tynecastle.

Willie, soon to be capped against the English League at Ibrox, struck the goal-standard also in Hearts' 3-0 win over Kilmarnock in the League Cup semi-final at Easter Road, so the Tynecastle team were in a Hampden Final for the third time in four years, this time to face Partick Thistle.

Willie is recalled to first-team duty.

Coincidentally, they warmed up for the occasion with a relatively easy, 2-0 League win over the Firhill side at Tynecastle, one of their goals going to Jimmy Wardhaugh who was wearing Alfie's old number 8 jersey.

But Jimmy had the accustomed number 10 on his back when, the following week, Dave Mackay led Hearts out at Hampden in front of a 60,000 crowd. Hearts' team that day, October 25, 1958, was: Marshall, Kirk, Thomson, Mackay, Glidden, Cumming, Hamilton, Murray, Bauld, Wardhaugh and Crawford.

E

As early as the third minute, when Willie scored the first of his two goals, it was evident that Hearts had the winning of the Cup. Jimmy Murray scored the first of his two goals after only eight minutes, by which time nobody was in much doubt that the trophy would go to the east of Scotland rather than the north of Glasgow.

Johnny Hamilton, for whom Blackpool had made an enquiry only a couple of weeks earlier, scored Hearts' fifth goal, just 10 minutes after half-time, to emphasise the measure of their superiority. It was yet another memorable day for the Tynecastle players for whom winning trophies had become a happy habit.

Willie was then being tipped to play for Scotland in a full international against Northern Ireland but, as so often before, the forecast proved to be ill-founded. Matt Busby, who had taken over as Scotland manager and demanded a say in selection, preferred the Anglo, David Herd, as a partner for the precocious youngster, Denis Law.

The distinguished Busby, by the way, had been openly critical a couple of years earlier of Scotland's selection system, saying that if the SFA's seven selectors ever struck success with their sides it would only be by accident.

Willie Bauld had undoubtedly suffered by the system. Although he was not short of admirers on the Selection Committee, one of whom had once described him as 'a genius', he could rarely convince them all at the one time of his international capabilities.

His style had always been what might now be described as 'laid back' but sceptics thought him lazy. As Tommy Walker once said, 'I know that Willie could give the impression of being, how can we say, unindustrious. Maybe that was a reason why he did not get more recognition by Scotland. But we all knew what he was doing. Willie was a great player, wonderful really.'

In contrast, nobody was ever in any doubt about Jimmy Wardhaugh's commitment. Alex Young, a great admirer of his, remarked, 'Jimmy could run, run, run — as the modern midfield players are demanded to do. It must have been very tiring for him but he had great stamina.'

Jimmy was still running when he scored against Hearts' bogey team of the previous season, Clyde, to help claim a 2-2 draw at

After the League Cup victory over Partick Thistle at Hampden in 1958, Dave Mackay proudly shows off the trophy. Beside him on the right are Willie Bauld and Jimmy Wardhaugh.

Tynecastle. It was a result which kept the champions two points ahead of Motherwell at the top of the League as the winter of 1958/59 approached.

Old Twinkle-toes then scored twice in a 5-1 win over Falkirk but a break in Hearts' resolve saw them lose 3-2 to Kilmarnock the following Saturday, despite a late goal by Willie.

Hearts' chance of retaining the title did not appear to be greatly jeopardised by that defeat. Indeed, they recovered from it in convincing fashion with a stunning 5-1 victory over Aberdeen at Tynecastle in the first week of December.

Willie scored three of their goals and Jimmy Murray the other two. Or was it the other way about? Only seconds before half-time, the two players climbed to head the same ball. Both claimed the resultant goal but, on the toss of a coin in the full-time dressing room, Willie was awarded the credit!

Hearts still had a two-point lead in the League at that point, Rangers having emerged as their closest rivals. The confrontation between the two at Ibrox in mid-December was likely to have a considerable bearing on the outcome of the Championship — and Hearts were destined to give their worst performance of the season, losing by a sickening 5-0.

The inspirational Dave Mackay had been out since the Aberdeen match, which obviously didn't help Hearts' cause at Ibrox. They were also without Jimmy Milne whose place at centre-half went to a rookie called Robertson.

But Milne at least was back in time for Celtic's visit to Tynecastle, a fixture which cost Hearts another valuable point. When, two days after Christmas, they were held to another draw at Dunfermline in the absence of both Willie and Dave, they had slipped to third position in the League, two points behind Rangers.

In short, 1958 could have had a happier ending for Hearts whose old friend Alfie Conn was still wrestling with bad luck at Raith Rovers. His initial bout of flu had been followed by jaundice as well as ankle and knee injuries, limiting his appearances to a mere two in the three months since he had departed from Tynecastle.

One newspaper labelled him as Scotland's most expensive player, a man who had cost Raith Rovers £1,500 a game by that point.

The new year began as ominously as the old one had finished, Hearts losing 3-1 to Hibs at Tynecastle. Neither Willie nor Jimmy was fit and played no part in the slender 3-2 win at Airdrie on January 3 which Hearts hoped would arrest their bad run.

Alas, it did not, for, after an interruption by adverse weather, Hearts resumed their stuttering League challenge by losing 4-1 to the unfashionable Stirling Albion at Tynecastle. Oddly, Willie Bauld was listed at outside-left that day and, dispensing with subtlety, the *Sunday Post* described him as 'a complete misfit'.

Their report added, 'Alex Young excepted, Hearts' forwards blundered from one futility to another.' More worryingly, the League table showed that the ailing champions had now slipped 6 points behind leaders, Rangers, with the young Ian St. John's Motherwell now looking a better bet to catch them.

There could be little doubt that Dave Mackay's absence had much to do with Hearts' lamentable lapse and, sadly, he was not to play many more games for them.

December 1958. Tommy Walker introduces Willie Bauld to the Duke of Gloucester before Hearts' 5-1 victory over Aberdeen at Tynecastle.

Hearts welcomed the start of the Scottish Cup as a timely distraction, Queen of the South being cleared from their path in a 3-1 win at Palmerston where a bloodstained Johnny Hamilton claimed most credit.

When the same wee winger upstaged Willie Bauld and Jimmy Wardhaugh in a subsequent 1-0 League win over Dundee, Hearts reportedly rejected a £10,000 bid from Bristol City for his services. The English club apparently turned their attention then to Alex Young but Tommy Walker told them 'Never, never, never.'

Hearts were duly beckoned back to Ibrox in the Cup, only to lose 3-2 despite an early goal by Dave Mackay who had returned to fitness at last. Neither Willie nor Jimmy, who were about to be stricken again by injuries, played well and, to compound the former's frustration, he was cautioned for a coarse shoulder charge on Rangers goalkeeper, George Niven.

So, left with only the Championship to play for, Hearts narrowly overcame Raith Rovers for whom a fit Alfie Conn was the only one of the erstwhile Trio on view. He scored Raith's goal in a 2-1 defeat with a typical shot from outside the box.

Hearts were nine points off the League lead, with two games in hand, and they contrived to cope with the continuing absences of both Willie and Jimmy by improvising with such as George Thomson at inside-forward.

A talented and versatile footballer, he did rather well in that role, scoring a hat-trick at Third Lanark as well as a single against Queen of the South which helped Hearts to an important, if unspectacular, 2-1 win.

But the Tynecastle side's revival was instantly threatened by the stunning and arguably unnecessary sale of Dave Mackay to Spurs for £32,000. He had no inkling of the London side's interest in him, nor did the Tynecastle fans.

He was a great loss to Hearts, Willie Bauld having observed that their sequence of successes, starting with the League Cup victory of 1954, had virtually coincided with Mackay's introduction to the side.

Yet, even without their captain as well as Willie and Jimmy, the Edinburgh side contrived to stay in touch with League leaders, Rangers, by beating Falkirk with a couple of goals by new signing, Bobby Rankin.

There were murmurs of discontent from Ibrox around that time that their possible League decider against Hearts at Tynecastle on April 11 coincided with Scotland's match at Wembley. They, if not Hearts, expected to forfeit a player or two to the international team.

In the event, they lost full-back Eric Caldow. They also lost the Tynecastle match — by 2-0 with John Cumming and Bobby Rankin scoring the home side's goals. But Rangers needed only one point from their remaining game, against Aberdeen at Ibrox, to secure the title, and Hearts probably thought they would get it without problem.

Thus, it is not too difficult to imagine Hearts' chagrin when they emerged from a 2-1 defeat by Celtic at Parkhead to learn that Rangers had lost by a similar margin.

Rangers were champions only by default, finishing two points ahead of Hearts whose total of goals for and against was identical to their own. In other words, had Hearts won by any score on that last day of the season they would have retained the title which their brilliant play had earned them a year earlier.

They must have felt as desolate as did their Tynecastle successors in 1986 when the League was lost to Celtic in equally agonising circumstances. Hitchcock could not have written a crueller ending to their script for season 1958/59.

Willie and Jimmy carried their despondency all the way to Australia on a close-season tour, although it may be fair to assume that they cheered up once they got there. Fit again after missing much of the run-in to the Championship, they indulged themselves in the goals which Hearts fired past hapless Aussie opposition.

It was while they were winning matches by such outlandish scores as 7-1 and 9-1 that the Edinburgh players learned that an old adversary, Gordon Smith, had been freed by Hibs. The word was that he would join Dundee but, possibly, Tommy Walker thought differently . . . .

CHAPTER TEN

Trio Minus Two

Gordon Smith nursed an ankle injury during the summer of 1959 and Tommy Walker nursed the desire to bring him across the city to Tynecastle, fitness permitting.

The Gay Gordon, as the debonair Hibs winger was known, duly signed for Hearts in August, and was to prove hugely influential, but manager Walker was rather less keen on seeing Jimmy Wardhaugh going in the opposite direction, to Easter Road.

Jimmy, a good tourist in Australia, had returned to Edinburgh to hear the rumour that Hibs as well as Dundee wanted to sign him and, after being left out of a League Cup tie against Kilmarnock, both he and Ian Crawford asked for transfers. Speculation that Jimmy was, indeed, bound for Easter Road was immediately stoked but Hearts, who fancied their chance of retaining the trophy, insisted that nobody was for sale.

Their reaction inspired a disgruntled Hibs fan to write to Tommy Walker on the following lines: 'When Hearts were in need, we gave you Jim Souness who helped you win the League Cup in 1954. Then we gave you Ian Crawford who won the Scottish Cup for you in 1956. Now you have Gordon Smith but you won't give us Jimmy Wardhaugh to steady the youngsters in our side. Why?'

Tommy Walker responded to the now ceaseless rumours by announcing publicly that there had been no bid from Hibs for Jimmy and, had there been, Hearts would have looked upon it sympathetically. So Jimmy seemed to be stuck at Tynecastle, like it or not . . .

Willie Bauld seemed happier with his lot, having made a fine start to the season by scoring in the Edinburgh Select's 4-3 win over Newcastle as well as Hearts' League Cup matches, both home and away, against Kilmarnock.

Gordon Smith was in the side for the second of these ties, making up a forward line of Smith, Young, Bauld, McFadzean and Hamilton. But injury soon forced Willie to the sidelines with the result that both he and Jimmy were spectators as Hearts began to build up their momentum for the season.

Having qualified from their League Cup section and beaten Motherwell on a 7-3 aggregate in the quarter-finals, they soon pushed to the top of the League with wins over Dunfermline, Ayr United and Airdrie.

Willie was then returning to fitness but he did not feature in the amazing 9-3 win over hapless Cowdenbeath in the semi-final of the Cup at Easter Road or, as luck dictated, the Final against Third Lanark on October 24.

Hearts, the trophy holders, fielded an attack of Smith, Crawford, Young, Blackwood and Hamilton that day at Hampden, Young and Hamilton scoring in their 2-1 win. But Willie, like Jimmy, was awarded a medal to mark his earlier good deeds in the tournament which now seemed to be Hearts' speciality.

In the wake of Hearts' latest success, neither Willie nor Jimmy could expect to be reinstated to the League side and, after victories over Rangers and Partick Thistle had been recorded, Jimmy's departure from Tynecastle was announced.

Dunfermline had offered £2,000 for him and Hearts believed that they and he had enjoyed his best years. Sadly, the most outstanding goal-scorer in their history was allowed to leave without so much as a cheerio from the directors.

Jimmy felt hurt and deflated when he walked out of Tynecastle with his boots under his arm. He had given Hearts 13 years of sterling service and scored an all-time club record number of goals: 375. Willie was just as sad to see him go.

They were as friendly off the field as they were on it, their families gathering regularly at one or the other's homes. Willie was often heard to remark that Hearts were wrong to allow Jimmy to leave and, in subsequent years, privately advocated that they should take him back as manager.

Indeed, nearer the end of his own career, Willie told a mutual friend that if Hearts made Jimmy manager, he would volunteer for the job of coach.

Jimmy duly made his debut for Dunfermline, who were near the foot of the table, against Celtic and scored a fine goal in the East End Park side's 4-2 defeat. The same day, Alfie Conn and a youngster called Willie Wallace scored in Raith Rovers' 4-2 win over Hibs.

But Willie Bauld was still blacked out of the picture at Tynecastle as Hearts beat Kilmarnock by 3-1 to push four points ahead of Rangers in the Championship. They stretched that lead to six points the following week when their 3-1 win at Aberdeen coincided with Alfie's Raith, including Jimmy Baxter, beating Rangers by 3-2 at Ibrox.

Alfie, free of injury and illness, was on a good run then, striking two goals in the same number of minutes in a 5-1 win at Pittodrie. Hearts were then seven points clear in the League but they stumbled into December, losing to St. Mirren and Motherwell in successive matches.

Willie featured in the second of these and held his place for the following Saturday when he was in opposition to Alfie and John Urquhart at Tynecastle. He was rated star man, too, as Hearts got back to their winning ways by beating Raith 4-1.

Gordon Smith and Willie then claimed top ratings for their performances in a 3-0 victory over Dundee which propelled the Tynecastle team into 1960 still three points ahead of Rangers. Jimmy Wardhaugh's Dunfermline were struggling in third bottom position but Alfie's Raith were respectably placed in mid-table.

Hearts fans truly believed that the new year would be a happy one when the team followed up a stunning 5-1 win over Hibs, in which Alex Young scored a hat-trick, with a 3-1 win against Celtic in which Willie scored once.

But those same supporters began to doubt their judgement as Hearts were held to a 2-2 draw against Dunfermline who were without Jimmy Wardhaugh. Hearts trailed by 2-0 until the 80th minute when George Thomson scored a penalty. Willie, who had

had a quiet game, was then thwarted by a brilliant save by Dunfermline's Eddie Connachan before Alex Young equalised in the last minute with what was Hearts' 100th goal of the season.

Still, Hearts contrived to keep their League rivals at arm's length as they pushed Stirling Albion aside in a 4-0 win at Tynecastle with two goals by Willie. But they began to stumble again, losing a point at Ayr United and another to Motherwell at home after Ian St. John scored in the final minute to cancel out a first-half goal by Willie.

The Scottish Cup had begun on a remarkable note by then, Joe Baker's brother Gerry scoring 10 goals for St. Mirren in their 15-0 victory over the hapless students of Glasgow University.

Bad weather caused Hearts' opening tie against Kilmarnock to be postponed twice. But they were held to a 1-1 draw when it was eventually played and beaten 2-1 in a replay.

Their early exit from the tournament merely strengthened their resolve to win the Championship for the second time in three seasons and, without the help of Willie Bauld, they beat Third Lanark by 4-1 at Cathkin.

Still without Willie, they beat Rangers 2-0 at Tynecastle to put an end to the Ibrox side's challenge. Killie had emerged as Hearts' sternest rivals by that point and contrived to beat them 2-1 at Rugby Park to move within five points to the leaders with two less games played.

Alas, poor Jimmy Wardhaugh's Dunfermline were still labouring to avoid relegation although the news that Jock Stein might take over as manager may have given them some belated hope of survival!

Hearts knew that they could not afford to stumble against Aberdeen at Tynecastle, their fourth last match of the Championship, and, with Willie back in place of Alex Young, they did not. Clinging to an early lead registered by Jim McFadzean, Hearts had less than 10 minutes to play when Willie headed in a cross by Gordon Smith. Almost immediately, the King provided a grateful Ian Crawford, who had renewed his transfer request, with the chance to make the score 3-0.

Killie remained in relentless pursuit, beating local rivals, Ayr United, by 3-1 to stretch their unbeaten run of matches to a creditable 20.

Scotland's annual match with England was imminent and it was amusing to note that Dave Mackay's place was in doubt for what the Scottish Selectors seemed to regard as an offence bordering on treachery.

Bad enough that he should have agreed a few weeks earlier to turn out for the English League against the Scottish League at Highbury. Much worse that he should have left himself open to accusations of using over-robust tactics against his fellow-countrymen!

But while John Cumming and Alex Young had both lodged sound claims for selection by Scotland at Hampden, and duly played there, Hearts remained preoccupied with the ambition of winning the League.

Killie were five points behind with one game less played when Hearts, whose goal average was infinitely superior, went to Paisley in search of two points or even one to take the title.

It proved to be a fascinating match but sore on Hearts' nerves as St. Mirren pushed into the lead on four occasions before Gordon Smith gathered the ball in the last minute. He passed to Ian Crawford who, in turn, supplied Willie Bauld. Clearly the calmest man at Love Street, Willie rolled the ball forward a yard or so, then rattled it into St. Mirren's net to claim a 4-4 draw.

Kilmarnock having been held to a 1-1 draw by Rangers at Ibrox, the Paisley result was all Hearts needed to proclaim themselves champions again. Theirs had been another marvellous effort, rounded off by a superb one from Willie.

His 17 League appearances that season had yielded 10 goals, including a hat-trick against Third Lanark. It was a handsome contribution from a man who, a couple of years earlier, had appeared to be headed towards the exit at Tynecastle. He was rewarded with a rest, Hearts leaving him out of their remaining League fixture, a 2-2 draw with Raith who were about to release an ageing Alfie.

Hearts, League Cup winners as well as Scottish champions, packed their bags that summer and headed once more for North America, leaving John Cumming, Alex Young and Billy Higgins to go on tour with Scotland. Tommy Walker was duly awarded the OBE in recognition of Hearts' outstanding successes since 1954 and Willie Bauld was still King.

The years go by, but still Willie is the King.

Privately, he had feared that he might be given a free transfer. Aged 32, he would not have believed anybody who told him that he still had two worthwhile seasons to serve with the club he had served with such distinction since 1948.

Never in their history, indeed, had Hearts had a finer servant than the man whose Tynecastle admirers used to sing:

'There's a team in Bonnie Scotland, their colours are maroon.
They have the finest centre that Scotland's ever known.
You can talk about your Reillys, your Buckleys and them all.
But you ought to hear the roar go up when Willie's on the ball.'

CHAPTER ELEVEN

Willie's Final Fling

Another Championship had been won by Hearts since Alfie Conn and Jimmy Wardhaugh disappeared down Gorgie Road but the doughty deeds of the Terrible Trio made for memories which were worth reviving.

Thus, on a nostalgic night at Tynecastle in October, 1960, the Trio was re-formed for a testimonial match in the name of George Dobbie, formerly of Third Lanark, Hearts and Raith Rovers and a man who had once described Willie as the 'complete player'.

Hearts and Raith were the teams in opposition, playing a 2-2 draw for a small but appreciative crowd of 6,600. Alfie, recruited from Gala Fairydean, reminded onlookers of his old skills by laying on his old side's first goal for Johnny Hamilton with a delightful dummy and pass.

Then Jimmy, the wily veteran of Dunfermline, set up Hearts' second goal for Ian Crawford. It was like an episode from the Good Old Days, one which slipped past all too quickly for the sentimentalists.

Willie's place in the regular Hearts team had become even more insecure by then, although predictably so. Youth had long since deserted him. But he was reportedly 'back at his best' when he played in a 2-1 League Cup victory over Motherwell in which soldier boy, Alex Young, scored twice.

He also helped Hearts get off to a flying start in the Championship again that season as they beat Hibs by 4-1 at Easter Road before the entire Tynecastle team suffered a dramatic loss of form.

It resulted in a succession of draws with Dunfermline, Airdrie and Dundee United and, despite sweeping changes by Tommy Walker, an ignominious defeat by Ayr United. During this luckless run, Hearts also lost on a 5-1 aggregate to Benfica in the European Cup which resulted in Willie and Gordon Smith being dropped.

Manager Walker publicly denied that team spirit was ailing although morale stood to be further undermined by rumours that Everton were chasing Alex Young. He played in Scotland's 2-0 defeat in Wales in the same week as Willie, having been reinstated to Hearts' attack, failed in a bold attempt to help the side avoid a 3-1 defeat by Rangers at Tynecastle.

Twice Willie drove in shots which appeared to beat Bobby Shearer who was deputising in goal for the injured Billy Ritchie. Twice Eric Caldow cleared off the line. Such was Hearts' luck at the time, such was Willie's.

The reigning champions had slipped into the lower half of the League by the time that they were held to a 1-1 draw with Clyde at Shawfield, a match which coincided with the revelation that Alex Young, as well as the talented George Thomson, could both leave for Everton.

Hearts duly collected £58,000 for these two and Tommy Walker set about the task of rebuilding the team which had served him so well, making more use of Willie's experience after the New Year.

Still, the team's form remained frustratingly inconsistent, a defeat by Dunfermline being followed by a 3-1 win over Airdrie in which Willie claimed the first goal. Then came a 3-0 defeat by Dundee United.

Jimmy Wardhaugh, incidentally, had slipped into Dunfermline's reserve team by then, making the odd appearance in the unlikely role of centre-half. Jock Stein revealed, 'I'd seen him playing there for Hearts' reserves once and noted that he exerted a tremendous influence on the young lads about him.'

Alfie, who had turned down the invitation to remain in the Scottish League with Morton, was still trying to cajole Gala Fairydean to greater things although their attempt to make an impression on the Scottish Cup that season ended in a defeat by fellow-borderers, Peebles Rovers.

Hearts began spectacularly in the same tournament, thrashing another non-League side, Tarff Rovers, by 9-0. But the King was not amongst their number. His position was occupied that day in January, 1961 by the versatile Danny Ferguson who impressed with a hat-trick. Willie was back for the later Cup rounds, however, helping Hearts to beat Kilmarnock and Partick Thistle before St. Mirren beat them 1-0 at the quarter-final stage.

According to the *Sunday Post*, he and Gordon Smith attempted every ploy known to them to cancel out Donny Kerrigan's first-half goal for the visiting Paisley side. None of them worked.

Willie had scored what was then a rare goal in an intervening League victory over Ayr United but Hearts continued their search for his successor, despatching Bobby Parker to have another look at the athletic George Smith of Partick Thistle.

They duly signed Maurice Elliott from Queen of the South although, in a subsequent 1-1 draw with Raith Rovers, they became convinced that the Starks Park forward, Willie Wallace, was the man they really needed.

Hearts' forward line had become almost unrecognisable by then, featuring players like David Johnstone from Nairn on one wing and Tommy Henderson on the other. But, by the end of the season when a huge clear-out was promised, Wallace had been bought in an attempt to strengthen their identity.

Hearts finished in eighth position which underlined the dramatic drop in their form from the previous season. Yet, while they appeared to have found Willie's true successor in Wallace, they were not of a mind to ask the King to abdicate.

Indeed, as season 1961-62 approached, Jack Harkness reported that, while there had been half-a-dozen offers for Willie, Tommy Walker insisted that he was not for sale.

'Our plans for the future include having two of our present-day players on our permanent, back-room staff,' Harkness quoted the manager as saying. 'These two are Willie Bauld and John Cumming who can bring up our youngsters in the Hearts' tradition.'

Willie, eventually denied such an opportunity, duly made what was to be his last appearance for the Edinburgh Select in an entertaining pre-season match which produced a glut of goals: 4 for the players of Hearts and Hibs and seven for Burnley.

He didn't score but he helped the talented young Easter Road player, Davie Gibson, to a hat-trick. In so doing, he seemed to confirm that Hearts could still make some use of his talents in the new season and they gave him an early call, fielding him at Wallace's shoulder in a League Cup tie against the latter's old team, Raith Rovers.

Hearts, doubtless influenced by their most recent European experience, had adopted a 4-2-4 system by then and they were asking a lot of the ageing Willie Bauld to adapt to it. Indeed, not too many of the team seemed to feel too comfortable in the new system although they reached the League Cup Final again, only to lose 3-1 in a replay with Rangers.

The recently-transformed Tynecastle team had progressed to the second round of the Fairs Cup by then. Willie, the most experienced player on their staff, was asked to help them advance still further but he was unable to oblige.

After Willie Polland had miskicked and invited Inter Milan to score at Tynecastle, Willie was branded for a glaring miss in front of goal. Hearts ended up losing by a 5-0 aggregate to the infinitely superior Italians.

The year drew to a close, however, with Willie reminding his thousands of fans that he had lost none of his rare heading ability when he rose above all challengers to knock in a Bobby Blackwood cross against Kilmarnock at Tynecastle.

So there was life in the old legs yet, more than enough to run Hibs ragged in a floodlit match at Easter Road in mid-January, postponed from Ne'erday, which Hearts won by a creditable 4-1.

Alex Cameron wrote in the *Scottish Daily Mail* of the 'maestro of Tynecastle' who laid on two goals for schoolboy Alan Gordon and one for Willie Wallace before helping himself to one in the last minute. 'The 16,000 crowd was generous in its acclaim for Bauld who, at 34, was the most thoughtful and skilled of the 10 fiery forwards on view,' the *Mail's* man added.

Alan Gordon recalled, 'It was my first Edinburgh derby but easy to play in because Willie was at my side. I seem to remember that my first goal was a left-foot shot from a through-ball by him and my second a header from his cross.

'He and I used to do a lot of heading practice together, at the

In his last Scottish Cup tie, Willie watches Alan Gordon score one of his three goals against Vale of Leithen. Willie himself was to score one in Hearts' tally of five.

Heriot Watt ground at Colinton when I got out of school in the afternoons. Gordon Marshall would go in goal and we would spend time crossing the ball to one another.

'I must have picked up a lot from him although I suspect that his own marvellous heading ability was instinctive and down to perfect timing.' Willie followed up that outstanding derby performance with a typical goal in a 3-2 win over Airdrie just three days later, his header from Danny Paton's corner arching agonisingly over the hands of the Airdrie 'keeper who had been distracted by Willie Wallace.

Then, in what was to prove his last Scottish Cup tie, he claimed one of Hearts' five goals against Vale of Leithen, Alan Gordon scoring three of the others.

Willie was enjoying his final fling, helping Hearts to cling to fifth-top position by laying on a goal for Danny Ferguson when he was recalled against St. Johnstone at Tynecastle in early March.

But a week before the Tynecastle side lost 3-2 at home to Falkirk to finish an unsatisfactory sixth, the newspapers carried the depressing but perhaps inevitable headline — 'BAULD FREED BY HEARTS.'

It was a stark announcement which coincided with Scotland's 2-0 victory over England at Hampden and one which came 12 years after his Scotland debut against the same opponents at the same venue.

Barely had the bad news registered than George Farm of Queen of the South offered him the chance to extend his celebrated career down at Palmerston. Highland League clubs coveted his expertise, too, although Willie joked that the north was too cold for his liking.

'I cannot say anything about my future just now although, if a good offer came from a good club, I would be tempted to take it,' he told reporters. 'I suppose I am a bit disappointed about being released by Hearts. Mind you, I have to admit that I'd expected a free for about three seasons now.'

The new season began with Willie having received no offer good enough to tempt him to return to football, and a Testimonial match was staged for him at Tynecastle on the first Monday of November, 1962.

Sheffield United, managed by an old friend of Tommy Walker's, John Harris, agreed to provide the opposition and, despite poor weather, some 15,000 of Willie's well-wishers turned out. It was considered a very good crowd in the circumstances.

The kick-off was delayed for more than two minutes as the King, wearing a soft hat for a crown, walked to the centre-circle to take his bow. He was duly presented with a cheque for around £2,800 — enough to buy a house in those days — but he didn't immediately spy the strings attached.

Sheffield's expenses had to be deducted from the proceeds. So, too, did bills for police and caterers. And, notoriously, there was the cost of the ball, around £8. Willie was left with some £1,700 and a grievance which was to linger for the rest of his life. This was no way for Hearts to treat royalty.

More than 12 years passed before he returned to Tynecastle, to see his eight-year-old nephew play the role of mascot before a

Hearts Chairman Wilson Strachan with Willie at his Testimonial in November 1962.

match with Kilmarnock. When he took his seat in the directors' box beside his old team-mate and captain, Bobby Parker, thousands stood to applaud him. The King was briefly back in residence.

Willie Bauld died on March 11, 1977, aged 49. Crowds of his admirers lined Gorgie Road in respectful silence as his funeral cortege passed by on its way to Warriston Crematorium.

Jimmy Wardhaugh, then a full-time journalist, was asked by many of his old Tynecastle colleagues to write a tribute. He chose not to eulogise the footballer whose gifts had been so obvious to all. Instead, he remembered the man.

'Willie was a quiet sort of person but always found time to talk to a youngster on the street, encourage a new signing or chat to an OAP who just wanted to say he had spoken to Willie Bauld,' Jimmy wrote. 'He was always fun to be with for he had his own special brand of pawky humour. Above all else, he was generous as his many friends will testify.'

Jimmy Wardhaugh died on January 2, 1978, aged 48. Had Willie still been alive, he would have remembered him just as fondly.

CHAPTER TWELVE

Magical Talents

Davie Laing explained in the opening chapter that the outstanding success of the Terrible Trio was due to the magical blend of their distinctive and contrasting talents.

Alfie was the strong, forceful inside-right who could hit the ball from any distance. Willie was the cerebral centre-forward or, as Alfie himself once put it, 'the brains of the outfit.' Jimmy was the great grafter, the inside-left with the twinkle in his toes.

Undoubedly, a unique chemistry existed between the three players, a telepathy almost as a Rangers centre-half by the name of Willie Moles hinted in a letter of appreciation to the *Daily Record* shortly after Willie had retired.

He recalled a Rangers-Hearts match in which the Ibrox side had pushed into a two-goal lead, adding, 'Hearts were out of it until a long ball was played through the middle to Willie.

'I started to go for it, then hesitated when Willie ran in the opposite direction. By the time I got going again, the ball had passed me, Jimmy Wardhaugh had bounced up from nowhere and scored. Hearts were then into top gear and won 3-2.'

Moles went on to say that critics had blamed his inexperience for the loss of the goal in question but he countered, 'I prefer to think that it was down to the genius of Willie Bauld.'

Others who saw Bauld from a different perspective, like Jack Harkness the writer, also testified to his 'genius' so Alfie and Jimmy must have been guided by some extraordinary force to read his thoughts. Therein, perhaps, lay the telepathy.

Certainly, the understanding they displayed on the field was not learned on the training ground as it might conceivably be now. Freddie Glidden recalled that they were not even coached as such. Nobody really was in those days although the trio practised plenty, none more so than Willie who would spend hours at a time perfecting his outstanding heading ability.

They also picked up some valuable tips about how the game should be played and Alfie is on record as saying that one of the most beneficial was passed on by Bobby Dougan who told them, 'Football is an easy game and should be played simply. The thing to do is get rid of the ball, then move into space to get it back again.' Sounds easy, doesn't it?

The celebrity which the Terrible Trio enjoyed remains unparalleled in Tynecastle history. Indeed, it may not be tinkering too much with the truth to suggest that no player with any Scottish club has been more revered than the charismatic Willie Bauld.

His memory is preserved by the Willie Bauld Memorial Club which meets regularly in Edinburgh and sponsors a boys' tournament in his name. His photograph still occupies a proud place in the guests' lounge at Tynecastle. Other pictures hang in hostelries in the vicinity of the ground.

This writer even knows of a Glasgow businessman whose house is a veritable shrine to the one they called the King. Willie, along with Alfie and Jimmy, made up Hearts' Royal Flush, the best hand that any club had to deal during the 1950s. Amazingly, Scotland never played the same hand.

In a *Daily Record* series entitled 'The King and I', Alfie noted that Jimmy and he played together in representative games and that Willie and Jimmy also played together. But never were they fielded as a trio.

Somebody once suggested that the reason why was that Hearts did not have a representative on the then seven-man selection committee although the truth may not have been quite so simple.

As the former secretary of the Scottish Football Association, Ernie Walker, explained much more recently, the selectors worked in curious ways . . .

When they sat down to pick a team, they would start at the

Always among the prizes . . . a happy picture of the Terrible Trio in their heyday.

beginning: goalkeeper. Somebody would propose his choice which would then go to a vote. Any counter-proposals for the position would also be voted upon until, by consensus, they had a goalkeeper.

By the same, protracted process, the selectors would then choose a right-back, left-back, right-half, centre-half, left-half, outside-right etc. But the point implied by Ernie Walker was that the balance of the team was rarely considered.

If it had been, it would have been well-nigh impossible for Conn, Bauld and Wardhaugh to avoid playing together and, fitness permitting, over several years at that. No wonder that Matt Busby said if the selectors ever fielded a consistently winning side, it would only be by accident.

Willie, of course, was denied many caps because of injury although rumours that he shied away from playing for Scotland were patently untrue. The fact was that it was always left to Hearts to decide if he was fit or not although Willie believed that he would have been letting down colleagues if he had taken the field when he was carrying an injury.

Critics also suggested that he was lazy, especially late in his career. But Alfie rejected this notion in the 'King and I' series, saying, 'Willie knew how to conserve his energies rather than waste them on lost causes.'

Jimmy never knew such a thing as a lost cause, which was a primary reason why he, Hearts' greatest scorer, claimed so many goals inside the penalty box, many of them late on in matches. Given that the modern game is more concerned than the old one was with work-rate, Jimmy's limitless energy would be a greatly valued commodity today.

Sadly, his ball-skills might not have been so treasured for he would have been encouraged to part with the ball quicker than was his wont. John Cumming used to joke that, when he played outside-left to Jimmy, 'there wasn't enough work in the position for me.'

The reason, he said, was that 'Jimmy wasn't too keen on parting with the ball once he got it!'

Alfie's game was simpler than Jimmy's although he could feint with the ball and wrong-foot an opponent by gliding effortlessly, deceptively inside him before having a shot. His shooting ability alone would guarantee his selection nowadays. Anybody who could hit the heavy, old ball with the power that he did could make a blur of the modern one.

The question of whether Willie Bauld would have been as good a player 35 years on is hardly worthy of debate. His youthful team-mate, Alex Young, implied that he was, in fact, years ahead of his time in his use of the first-time pass, for example.

Young recalled, too, that Willie was also completely two-footed, had superb vision and could head a ball with power and accuracy which nobody since has been able to match.

Another contemporary, Johnny Urquhart, testified that Willie could head a goal from any point in the penalty box, and Alfie swore he knew the secret: Willie's eyes were always wide open when he made contact with the ball.

Conn, Bauld and Wardhaugh were stars. They would shine as brightly today as they did in the 1950s. Indeed, they are still shining in the memories of the many who crowded on to the terraces of Tynecastle to be dazzled by the outstanding talents of the Terrible Trio.

Index